# THE
# LOST
# PRINCE

# About the Author

David Baldwin is a medieval historian who specialises in the later fifteenth century and who has long been fascinated by the enigma of Richard III. He is much in demand as a lecturer in these subjects, and has devised and taught courses for adults at Leicester University's Vaughan College and Northampton Centre for more than twenty years. His acclaimed biography, *Elizabeth Woodville: Mother of the Princes in the Tower*, was published in 2002.

ALSO BY DAVID BALDWIN

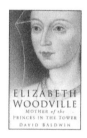

Elizabeth Woodville: Mother of the Princes in the Tower

£8.99 paperback

07509 3886 2

# THE
# LOST
# PRINCE

## THE SURVIVAL OF
## RICHARD OF YORK

DAVID BALDWIN

*Cover illustrations*: *Front*: Detail from The Princes Edward and Richard in the Tower by Sir John Everett Millais, 1878 (Royal Holloway, University of London/Bridgeman Art Library); *Rear*: Richard, Duke of York, garter stall plate at St George's, Windsor (Geoffrey Wheeler).

First published 2007
This edition published 2016 by

The History Press
The Mill, Brimscombe Port
Stroud, Gloucestershire, GL5 2QG
www.thehistorypress.co.uk

British Library Cataloguing in Publication Data.
A catalogue record for this book is available from the British Library.

ISBN 978 0 7509 7856 9

Typesetting and origination by The History Press
Printed in India

# Contents

# List of Illustrations

# List of Illustrations

All illustrations are © Geoffrey Wheeler unless otherwise stated.

# Table Showing the York, Lancaster and Tudor Genealogies

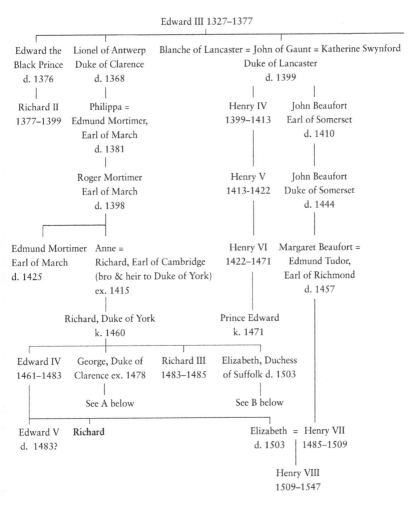

A. Edward, Earl of Warwick (ex. 1499). Margaret, Countess of Salisbury (ex. 1541).
B. John, Earl of Lincoln (k. 1487). Edmund, Earl of Suffolk (ex. 1513). Richard (k. 1525). Other sons & daughters.

# Time Chart of the Principal Events of English History during the Period Covered by this Book

## 1455–1461
The first phase of the Wars of the Roses. A series of battles fought between King Henry VI, his wife, Queen Margaret of Anjou, and supporters of the House of Lancaster against a faction of the nobility led by Richard, Duke of York, who ultimately claims to be the rightful king.

## 30 December 1460
Richard of York is killed at Wakefield. His son, Edward, Earl of March, is proclaimed king by 'Warwick the Kingmaker' in March 1461. Edward defeats the Lancastrians at Towton (Yorkshire) on Palm Sunday (29 March) and reigns as Edward IV, the first king of the House of York.

## 1 May 1464
Edward IV secretly marries Elizabeth Woodville, a daughter of Lord Rivers, to the consternation of many of his subjects who expect him to choose a foreign princess who would bring England a dowry and the goodwill of her country. The endowment of the new queen's numerous family is one of several factors that undermines the friendship between the King and the Earl of Warwick.

## Autumn 1469–March 1470
Warwick stirs up Robin of Redesdale's rebellion and the Lincolnshire rebellion, primarily to demonstrate to Edward that

he cannot manage without him. His success in the former allows him to execute several senior Woodvilles and even hold the King prisoner for a time; but defeat in the latter obliges him to flee to France, taking with him Edward's brother and his own son-in-law, George, Duke of Clarence.

*July–October 1470*
In France, Warwick is reconciled with the deposed Queen Margaret, and agrees to invade England on behalf of the House of Lancaster. Edward, deserted by some of his forces (including Warwick's brother, John, Marquess Montagu), is driven into exile in Burgundy. Henry VI is brought out of the Tower of London (where he has languished since 1464) and restored as king.

*2 November 1470*
Edward, Prince of Wales (King Edward's eldest son and the elder of the 'Princes in the Tower'), is born in sanctuary.

*14 March 1470*
King Edward returns from exile and, after being reconciled with his brother Clarence, defeats and kills Warwick and Montagu at the battle of Barnet (14 April). He completes his recovery of his kingdom by defeating Queen Margaret and her western Lancastrian army at the battle of Tewkesbury (4 May). King Henry's only son is slain at Tewkesbury, and Henry himself dies mysteriously in the Tower of London soon afterwards.

*17 August 1473*
**King Edward's second son, Prince Richard, is born at Shrewsbury.**

*28 May 1474*
Prince Richard is created Duke of York. At about this time William Caxton produces the first printed book in English, *The Recuyell of the Historyes of Troye*, in Bruges.

*June–September 1475*
King Edward invades France but is bought off with a large annual pension and the engagement of his eldest daughter to the Dauphin at the Treaty of Pecquigny.

*1476*
William Caxton sets up his printing press at Westminster, and prints *The Dictes or Sayings of the Philosophers* the following year.

*7 February 1477*
Prince Richard is created Duke of Norfolk prior to marrying Anne, daughter and heiress of the last Mowbray duke, on 15 January 1478.

*18 February 1478*
The Duke of Clarence is executed, although his offences, born of frustration and disappointment, do not appear to warrant the ultimate penalty.

*9 April 1483*
King Edward dies at the comparatively young age of 40. His son, Prince Edward, succeeds as Edward V, but the late King's surviving brother, Richard, Duke of Gloucester, stages a coup that ensures his own appointment as Protector during the boy's minority.

*13–26 June 1483*
Duke Richard accuses William, Lord Hastings, and other lords loyal to Edward V of plotting against him. He is informed by Robert Stillington, Bishop of Bath and Wells, that when King Edward married Elizabeth Woodville he was already precontracted to another lady, and that all his brother's children by Elizabeth are therefore illegitimate and unable to succeed. Elizabeth, who had fled into sanctuary when she received word

of Richard's first coup, is compelled to surrender Prince Richard to him (16 June), and the boy is sent to join his elder brother in the Tower. Duke Richard is declared the rightful heir of the House of York and becomes king, as Richard III, on 26 June.

### October 1483
King Richard's ally, the Duke of Buckingham, leads an unsuccessful rebellion to restore Edward V to the throne. The rebels hear a rumour that the young King is no more and transfer their allegiance to Richard's Lancastrian rival, the exiled Henry Tudor.

### Christmas Day 1483
Henry Tudor swears an oath in Rennes Cathedral to marry Princess Elizabeth of York (Edward V's and Prince Richard's sister) when he is able to defeat King Richard, thereby uniting the two rival branches of the royal family.

### August 1485
Henry Tudor invades England with a small force and, remarkably, defeats and kills King Richard at the battle of Bosworth (22 August). Henry becomes king as Henry VII and marries Elizabeth of York in January 1486. Prince Arthur, their first son, is born on 20 September.

### June 1487
A group of Yorkist dissidents, including the Earl of Lincoln (Richard III's nephew), and Francis, Viscount Lovel, the late King's chamberlain, mount a rebellion against Henry, but are defeated at Stoke by Newark on 16 June.

### 1491–1499
Perkin Warbeck appears in Ireland claiming to be Prince Richard of York. He resembles Edward IV, his alleged father,

behaves plausibly, and is recognised by several European heads of state when they wish to make trouble for Henry; but he is unable to say how he escaped from the Tower or name any witnesses who would verify his story. He is captured after the failure of his third abortive invasion of England in 1497 and executed with the Earl of Warwick (the Duke of Clarence's son and the most obvious Yorkist rival to Henry) two years later.

*May–June 1497*
Cornishmen led by Michael Joseph, a blacksmith, Thomas Flamank, a lawyer, and Lord Audley rebel against taxation and march on London but are defeated at Blackheath (17 June). At about this time the Cabots reach Nova Scotia and return with reports that lead to the development of the Newfoundland fisheries.

*November 1501*
Prince Arthur is married to the Spanish princess Catherine of Aragon.

*April 1502*
Prince Arthur dies, followed by his mother, Queen Elizabeth of York, in February 1503.

*1499–1509*
King Henry enjoys greater peace and security after Warbeck's execution, but suffers increasingly from illness. He dies, aged 52, on 21 April 1509, and is succeeded by Henry, his only surviving son. Sebastian Cabot leads an expedition to search for the North-West Passage to Asia (1509), but turns back when confronted by ice.

*11 June 1509*
Henry VIII marries Catherine of Aragon.

*4 May 1513*
Edmund de la Pole, the slain Earl of Lincoln's brother, known as the 'White Rose', is executed.

*1513*
English armies defeat the French at the battle of the Spurs (16 August), and the Scots at Flodden (9 September), killing the Scottish king, James IV.

*24 December 1515*
Thomas Wolsey, having made himself indispensable to the young King Henry, becomes Chancellor of England.

*18 February 1516*
The future Queen Mary is born to the King and Queen at Greenwich Palace.

*June 1520*
Henry VIII meets King Francis I of France at the 'Field of the Cloth of Gold'.

*May 1521*
Edward Stafford, Duke of Buckingham (the son of Richard III's Buckingham), is arrested and executed for allegedly promoting his own claim to the throne.

*11 October 1521*
Henry is given the title 'Defender of the Faith' by Pope Leo X.

*14 February 1525*
Battle of Pavia. The French army is heavily defeated by the forces of the Emperor Charles V in Lombardy. King Francis I is captured and Richard de la Pole, the last of the sons of the Duke and Duchess of Suffolk to claim the English Crown, killed.

*1525*

William Tyndale translates the New Testament into English. The authorities try to prevent it from being distributed in England and copies are publicly burnt at St Paul's Cathedral in 1527.

*Spring 1527*

Henry VIII, troubled by his lack of a male heir, begins to consider annulling his marriage to Catherine of Aragon. A great debate ensues in which Leviticus 18: 16 and 20: 21, which apparently forbids marriage with a deceased brother's widow, is pitted against Deuteronomy 25: 5, which appears to require a surviving brother to marry his widowed sister-in-law and 'raise up seed for his brother'.

*22 September 1529*

Wolsey is dismissed as chancellor after failing to persuade the Pope to end Henry's marriage. Thomas More is appointed in his stead.

*1531*

The appearance of Halley's Comet causes widespread panic.

*25 January 1533*

Henry secretly marries Anne Boleyn, his already pregnant mistress. Archbishop Cranmer declares his marriage to Catherine null and void on 23 May. Anne is crowned queen on 1 June.

*May 1534*

Convocation declares that the Pope has no more authority in England that any other foreign bishop, and Parliament formally recognises Henry as head of the English Church (November).

*15 January 1535*

Thomas Cromwell, appointed Henry's secretary (1533) and Master of the Rolls (1534), begins to exercise supreme authority over the Church as Vicar General. Bishop John Fisher is beheaded for refusing to take the oath of assent to the Act of Succession on 22 June, followed by Thomas More on 6 July. (Both are prepared to recognise Anne as queen and her children as Henry's heirs, but will not accept the implied repudiation of the authority of the Pope.)

*19 May 1536*

Queen Anne is beheaded after being convicted of adultery – an event perhaps not unconnected with her failure to give Henry a son. The King is immediately betrothed to Jane Seymour, whom he marries on 30 May.

*October 1536*

The dissolution of the smaller monasteries gives rise to the 'Pilgrimage of Grace', an insurrection fomented in the northern and eastern counties with the aim of compelling the King to reverse the recent religious changes. Henry, outnumbered, dissembles, but then punishes the rebels severely after he has persuaded them to disband their forces.

*12 October 1537*

Prince Edward is born. Queen Jane, his mother, dies twelve days later.

*5 September 1538*

Cromwell instructs parish clergy to keep records of baptisms, weddings and burials.

*9 December 1538*

Execution of the 'Yorkist' Henry Pole, Lord Montague (brother of Cardinal Reginald Pole, Henry's sternest critic, and a grandson of the Duke of Clarence), followed by that of Henry Courtenay, Marquess of Exeter, a grandson of Edward IV, on 9 January 1539. Their young sons are sent to the Tower.

*April 1539*
The 'Great (English) Bible', financed by Cromwell and edited by Miles Coverdale, receives royal approval.

*May 1539*
Parliament passes an Act dissolving the greater monasteries, notwithstanding earlier favourable references to them. The abbots of Colchester, Reading and Glastonbury are charged with treasonable activities and executed in the autumn.

*6 January 1540*
Henry marries Anne of Cleves – and divorces her on 9 July. Thomas Cromwell is created Earl of Essex on 18 April (notwithstanding the failure of the Cleves marriage), but is executed, brought down by his enemies, who have managed to persuade the King that he is a heretic and traitor, on 28 July. Henry marries Catherine Howard privately the same day.

*27 May 1541*
Execution of Margaret, Countess of Salisbury (the Duke of Clarence's daughter), after nearly two years' imprisonment. She suffers more as a substitute for her exiled son Cardinal Pole than for any crime she has committed herself.

*June 1541*
Henry becomes king, as opposed to 'lord', of Ireland, confirming his headship of the Irish Church.

*13 February 1542*

Catherine Howard executed after committing adultery with the courtiers Thomas Culpeper and Francis Dereham. Henry marries Catherine Parr, his last wife, on 12 July 1543.

*23 November 1542*

English forces defeat the Scots at Solway Moss. James V dies three weeks later, leaving his throne to his week-old daughter Mary Queen of Scots.

*19 July 1545*

The warship *Mary Rose* suddenly heels over and sinks in the Solent. Henry watches from Southsea Castle as 700 men are drowned.

*28 January 1547*

Henry VIII dies. The 9-year-old Edward VI succeeds and is crowned on 16 February.

*10 September 1547*

The Duke of Somerset crushes Scottish resistance to the new government at the battle of Pinkie.

*Summer 1549*

Religious protests in the north, the west country and Norfolk ('Kett's Rebellion'), sparked by the introduction of the *Book of Common Prayer* and compounded by economic grievances, are defeated by the aristocracy's reluctance to upset the existing settlement.

*22 December 1550*
**Richard Plantagenet dies at Eastwell in Kent.**

*6 July 1553*

Edward VI dies. The Duke of Northumberland's attempt to preserve and further the cause of the Protestant reformation by promoting the claims of Lady Jane Grey over those of the Catholic Princess Mary end in disaster and Mary becomes queen.

# Introduction

King Richard III is unquestionably the most maligned of all England's rulers, more so than either King John, who was suspected of having murdered his nephew Prince Arthur, or William Rufus, who was condemned by contemporaries for his abuse of the Church. He has been variously accused of complicity in the deaths of the Lancastrian King Henry VI and Henry's son Prince Edward in 1471, and in the execution of his own brother George, Duke of Clarence, seven years later. He had William, Lord Hastings, Anthony Woodville, Earl Rivers and several others beheaded in 1483, ostensibly because he feared they would resist his seizure of authority; and unkind rumours accused him of trying to poison his wife, Queen Anne, so that he could remarry and beget an heir. People inevitably feared the worst when Edward V and his younger brother disappeared into the Tower of London, and they were still 'missing, presumed dead' when Richard was slain at Bosworth in 1485.

Richard never sought to excuse or dispel any of these allegations, probably because he thought that to do so was both unkingly and unnecessary. He may (or may not) have been involved in the deaths of King Henry, Prince Edward and Clarence, but they all died in Edward IV's reign and Edward must bear the ultimate responsibility. The executions of Hastings, Rivers and the others were brutal and tyrannical but must be viewed in the context of the ruthlessness of the era; and the best medical opinion is that Queen Anne probably succumbed to tuberculosis, or 'consumption', after an illness lasting a few months. It is unlikely that Richard would be particularly remembered for any of these things if his reign had been long and reasonably successful (how many people did Henry VIII, 'Bluff King Hal', kill, for example?), but the murder of children, and particularly of a child who had been a king, was an entirely different matter. No one knows what became of the two 'Princes', but it is this, more than any other factor, that has blighted the King's reputation for the past five hundred years and more.

The main question, then, is why did Richard not produce the two boys alive and confound his critics? The most obvious answer is that he, or someone else, had killed them, or that to do so would have restored them to the centre of attention in a way that was entirely unacceptable to him. Some writers have argued that, once they had been declared illegitimate, they were no longer a threat to him or to anyone; but a new parliament could always reverse the Acts of its predecessors and the so-called Buckingham's rebellion showed how the disaffected could turn even the possibility that the Princes were still living to their own advantage. The evidence that Richard himself ordered their deaths is late and unsatisfactory, and attempts to pin the crime on Buckingham – either with the King's knowledge or without it – have only added to the speculation. The Princes were assumed to be dead because they disappeared so completely, so effectively, that no other hypothesis was possible. But a king's sons could not simply vanish from royal custody without the authorities – together with close family members and servants – knowing or learning what had become of them, and the real question is not how few knew the answer to the mystery but how many? There would have been nothing to prevent these people from discussing the matter openly in later years if the Princes had died and passed into history, but it would have been a very different matter if both – or even one – of them had survived.

What follows may be partly or even wholly fiction: or it may be the solution to this, the most enduring of all historical mysteries. Such an admission may seem surprising, given that most books of this genre claim to be the 'last word' on whatever problem, or problems, their authors have decided to investigate, but such certainty is seldom justified unless a dramatic piece of new evidence has become available. Some years ago a writer estimated that no fewer that 152 individuals had been identified as 'Jack the Ripper' (the figure must be still greater now, of course), even though it is obvious that only one of them can be the culprit. The real killer may even be an obscure person who has not so far been linked to the murders (the most popular candidates are all suitably famous in one way or another), and new theories are unlikely to prove any more convincing, or enduring, than their predecessors. It is only very occasionally – as, for example, when some bones found near Ekaterinburg in Russia were identified as those of the last Tsar and some members of his family using genetic fingerprinting – that a mystery is solved with reasonable certainty, but even modern technology can take us only so far. Carbon-14 tests have shown that the Turin Shroud is a thirteenth or fourteenth-century forgery, but could any forger, no matter how gifted, have produced something which defied all expert analysis for so long? If the samples tested came (for example) from a piece of material that had been used to repair the shroud in the medieval period, then the results would be accurate but would tell us nothing about the date of the original cloth.

So where does all this leave an investigation into a subject like the 'Lost Prince'? There is, of course, no document that proves conclusively that Edward IV's heirs were still living at some time after the autumn of 1483, and so there can be no certainty, or closure, in the sense in which the word is used above. What we do have, however, is a number – a considerable number – of clues which seem to point to the conclusion that something was being played out behind the scenes, something that had to be kept hidden because of the risk it posed to Henry VII and, to a lesser extent, his son. Sceptics may – and probably will – argue that these apparent hints in the sources are all unrelated coincidences and mean nothing; but every idea needs to be probed and tested before it can be dignified by the word 'considerable' or discarded. It is easy to pick holes in a theory, but often harder to put a better argument in its place.

On a purely practical note, there is an excellent case to be made for modernising spelling and punctuation when quoting from medieval documents, but I feel that something of the flavour of the period is lost if the random, sometimes quite prosaic, grammar used by contemporaries is abandoned entirely. I have therefore given extracts in the original (or, in the case of Latin, as rendered by the translator), but have added the modern equivalent of difficult or archaic words in brackets. The original punctuation has been followed except where this would seriously affect the sense.

I have, as usual, been helped by a number of people in researching this book and preparing it for publication, and would like to particularly mention Paul Coverley, branch archivist at the Colchester and North-East Essex branch of the Essex Record Office, Dr Richard Palmer, librarian and archivist at Lambeth Palace Library, and John Ashdown-Hill, Marilyn Garabet, Philippa Langley and Doug Weeks of the Richard III Society, who all provided information in response to my inquiries. Ann Wroe answered questions arising from her excellent book *Perkin: A Story of Deception*, and Geoffrey Wheeler provided illustrations and information culled from the Richard III Society's files of press cuttings. I am particularly grateful to Ann and Geoff for reading a draft of my text and for commenting upon it, but I take full responsibility for the theory and for any mistakes that none of us has noticed! Lastly, I would like to thank Christopher Feeney, senior commissioning editor at Sutton Publishing, for his interest in the project, my editor, Hilary Walford, and, as always, my wife Joyce for her constant encouragement and help.

David Baldwin
April 2006

You remember Chief Justice Crewe's famous question: 'Where is Bohun, where is Mowbray, where is Mortimer? Nay, which is more and most of all, where is Plantagenet? Gone in name, but not perhaps in blood. Somewhere those high strains are in the commonalty of England, for it is the commonalty that endures.'

(John Buchan, *The Blanket of the Dark*, 1931)

# ONE

## *The Mystery of the Princes*

The fate of the 'Princes in the Tower' is the most famous of all historical mysteries. It perplexed contemporaries much as it continues to puzzle modern writers, but no one has yet managed to discover what happened to the deposed King Edward V and Richard, Duke of York, his younger brother, after they were imprisoned in the Tower of London in the summer of 1483. Most books on the Princes are as long on background as they are short on answers,[1] and most conclude that they were killed by their uncle, Richard III, or perhaps by his ally Henry Stafford, Duke of Buckingham, or (less probably) by Henry VII. There is, of course, no proof that they were killed by anyone, and this book will argue that the younger boy survived and lived under an assumed name, in obscurity, until the middle of the sixteenth century. There can never be absolute certainty or there would hardly be a mystery in the first place; but the probability is that Richard III did not murder his nephews, and that the bones found in the Tower in 1674 and placed in an urn in Westminster Abbey are those of two other children whose names and origins will never be known.

The first problem that confronts any investigator into the Princes' disappearance is how knowledgeable contemporary writers with access to the court or court sources could *not* have known or discovered what had become of them. Edward V and his brother have always excited popular attention, and it is difficult to avoid the conclusion that both Richard III and Henry VII knew more about their disappearance than they chose to reveal to any but their most trusted counsellors. Both may have thought that a policy of 'least said, soonest mended' would best suit their purposes, and both would have sought to draw a veil over the matter if they knew that at least one of the boys was still living. Dead princes were a potential embarrassment, but a live prince, with a better claim to the throne than either of them, would have been a real danger and a closely guarded secret. Writers of histories were left to make what they could of it, and we must first see if anything can be gathered from the few conclusions they were able to reach.

The 'second continuation' of the *Croyland* (modern Crowland) *Chronicle* is one of the fullest and most detailed sources for the period, principally because its author served all three Yorkist kings in a senior capacity. He offered, or was invited, to add his memoirs to the rather poor efforts of the monks' own scrivener when he visited Croyland Abbey at the beginning of Henry VII's reign, and the result was a piece of first-rate historical writing containing many details that would otherwise be lost. We do not know his identity, although clues based on internal evidence point to John Russell, Bishop of Lincoln and Richard III's Chancellor, or John Gunthorpe, Dean of Wells and the King's Keeper of the Privy Seal, as the most likely candidates;[2] but there can be no doubt that he possessed inside information and would have known what was being said of the Princes in dark corners at court. He could easily have included something of this in his narrative, but all he chooses to tell us is that when the Duke of Buckingham turned against

King Richard in the autumn of 1483 (and presumably contemplated restoring young Edward), 'a rumour arose that King Edward's sons, by some unknown manner of violent destruction, had met their fate'.[3] A rumour is a rumour irrespective of how many are persuaded to believe it, and the Continuator nowhere else mentions the Princes or indicates whether he thought (or knew) that the story was accurate. Professor Hanham suggests that he may have felt embarrassed by the way in which he and others had failed to stand up to Richard after the Princes' friends, Earl Rivers and Lord Hastings, had been brutally executed;[4] but it is equally possible that he knew that at least one of the boys had outlived King Richard, and would not risk endangering him by a single word of 'loose talk'.

The second commentator who was well placed to learn the fate of the Princes was Henry VII's court historian Polydore Vergil. Vergil was born in Urbino, in Italy, about 1470, and came to England when his patron, Adriano Castelli, was appointed Bishop of Hereford in 1502. He brought with him a reputation as a humanist historian and man of letters, and the King asked him to research and write a history of England in about 1506. He spent the next seven years working on the project, and, although he could not match the Croyland writer's personal involvement in the events of the later fifteenth century, he made up for it by studying official documents and by consulting 'those who had often been employed in the highest business of state'.[5] His avowed aim was to be both truthful and impartial, but the critical part of the *Anglica Historia* is inevitably coloured by the interpretation that Henry VII and his ministers wished to place on the recent past. King Richard, he alleges, decided to rid himself of the Princes when he was at Gloucester at the beginning of August 1483, and sent instructions to this effect to Sir Robert Brackenbury, the constable of the Tower. Brackenbury delayed implementing the 'cruel' and 'horrible' order, hoping that the King would reconsider the matter; but, when word of his reluctance was communicated to Richard, he (Richard) 'anon commyttyd the charge of hastening that slawghter unto another, that is to say James Tyrrell, who, being forcyd to do the kings commandment, rode sorowfully to London, and, to the woorst example that hath been almost ever hard [heard] of, murderyd those babes of thyssew [the issue] royall'.[6]

Vergil's story is based on a confession allegedly made by Tyrell while he was in the Tower of London awaiting execution for other, unrelated, offences, in 1502.[7] It seemed to be the last word on the matter, but if the information had always been available why had the King not used it against the pretender Perkin Warbeck in the 1490s? Tyrell's admission of guilt would have been an excellent way of refuting Warbeck's claim that he was the younger of the two Princes, and it does not say much for Henry's intelligence services if Sir James had successfully concealed his part in the murders for nearly twenty years. The 'confession' no longer exists – perhaps it was never written down anyway – and it is possible that Tyrell, who had been close to Richard III and was now about to be silenced, was simply used as a scapegoat. The government may have decided that 'proof' of the Princes' deaths would help to deter future pretenders, and Vergil was obliged to follow the official 'line' when he came to write his version of the story. This would have cut against the grain – particularly if he knew that one of the boys was still living – and he concludes his account with the curious comment that 'with what kinde of death these sely [innocent] chyldren wer executyd yt is not certanely known'.[8] It beggars belief that Tyrell could have confessed without someone asking him how he had killed the boys, and it is just possible that Vergil is hinting (as far as he could in the circumstances) that what he was writing was not the answer to the mystery it claimed to be.

This brings us to two men who were not themselves courtiers (in the broadest sense of the word) when they wrote their commentaries, but who had access to knowledgeable court figures. The first, Dominic Mancini, was an Italian ecclesiastic whom Angelo Cato, King Louis XI of France's doctor and counsellor, sent to England to gather information, possibly in the summer or autumn of 1482. He was thus in London when Edward V was deposed by his uncle, although he appears to have left very shortly after 6 July 1483, when Cato recalled him and when his narrative ends. He may not have known English and would have relied on fellow Latin or Italian speakers to tell him what was happening; but one of his informants was almost certainly John Argentine, the young King's doctor. Mancini's story of how the two boys were deprived of their attendants and kept in closer confinement 'and day by day began to be seen more rarely behind the bars and windows, till at length they ceased to appear altogether' may be based on gossip, but he then tells us that Dr Argentine 'reported that the young king, like a victim prepared for sacrifice, sought remission of his sins by daily confession and penance, because he believed that death was facing him'.[9] It is usually assumed that Edward V knew that three of his recent predecessors, Edward II, Richard II and Henry VI, had all been murdered by their supplanters (irrespective of any assurances they had been given when they were deposed or forced to abdicate), and feared that his own demise was now inevitable. But, if Dr Argentine was attending him regularly, he was presumably in need of medical assistance, and could have witnessed enough illness and death in his short life to expect the worst. It is interesting that Argentine did not, according to Mancini, say that Prince Richard also expected to die in the near future, although it would have been pointless to kill the ex-king without also eliminating his heir apparent. Mancini wrote that he had 'seen many men burst forth into tears and lamentations when mention was made of him [Edward

V] after his removal from men's sight; and already there was a suspicion that he had been done away with'. But he could obtain no confirmation of this from Argentine, and was obliged to admit that, 'whether, however, he has been done away with, and by what manner of death, so far I have not at all discovered' when he reported to Cato on 1 December 1483.[10]

Thomas More, our second informed source, was only 7 years old when Richard III was killed at Bosworth and had not embarked on his distinguished career in royal service when he wrote his unfinished *History* of the King in 1513. Regrettably, he did not return to the subject after he became a senior minister and perhaps gained access to privileged information, but he had spent several of his boyhood years in the household of John Morton, Archbishop of Canterbury, one of the few men who enjoyed Henry VII's confidence and who almost certainly knew what had become of the Princes. Morton, who thought More a youth of great promise, may have hinted to him, almost teasingly, that there were certain things that must remain hidden; and this may be why More qualifies his otherwise full and apparently indisputable account of the boys' murder with the statement: 'I shall rehearse you the dolorous end of those babes, *not after every way that I have heard*, but after that way that I have so heard by suche men and by such meanes as me thinketh it wer hard but it should be true' (emphasis added).[11]

More wrote at the same time as Polydore Vergil, and, like Vergil, based his story on Sir James Tyrell's alleged confession. The difference is that More named the men whom Tyrell had employed to kill the Princes and described how they met their fate in graphic detail, information that was not, apparently, available to Polydore. It would be tempting to suppose that More had learned this from Morton, who died two years before Vergil arrived in England; but Morton's death also pre-dated Tyrell's confession, and it is hard to imagine a senior statesman regaling a teenager with state secrets. The probability is that, if

More ever heard any of this from Morton, it was designed to obfuscate the truth rather than reveal it, and More the eminent lawyer would not, arguably, have betrayed any real confidences his late master had imparted to him. He concludes his account of the Princes' fate with the words 'and thus as I have learned of them that much knew and litle cause had to lye'.[12] He appears, at first glance, to be assuring his readers that his account is based on sound evidence, but a more subtle interpretation would be that he does not vouch personally for its accuracy. His real aim was to warn 'of the evils which permeate a kingdom when tyranny is allowed to take the place of wise government and good order', as his modern editor has it,[13] and a dramatic story does not always tell the whole truth.

The Croyland writer, Vergil, Mancini and More were arguably best placed to know what had become of the Princes, but they were not the only contemporary and near-contemporary commentators to claim or suspect that they had been killed within a short time of Edward V's deposition. Most foreign observers thought that this was what had happened and placed the blame squarely on King Richard's shoulders. The French chancellor Guillaume de Rochefort, addressing the Estates General at Tours on 15 January 1484, reminded his hearers of how King Edward's children, 'already big and courageous, have been put to death with impunity, and the royal crown transferred to their murderer by the favour of the people', while his fellow courtier Philippe de Commines wrote in his *Memoirs* that the Duke of Gloucester 'killed Edward's two sons, declared his daughters bastards, and had himself crowned king'. The Castilian Diego de Valera informed Ferdinand and Isabella in March 1486 that 'it is sufficiently well known to your royal majesty that this Richard killed two innocent nephews of his to whom the realm belonged after his brother's life', and Casper Weinrich of Danzig wrote that 'later this summer [1483] Richard the king's brother seized power and had his brother's children killed and the queen secretly put away . . .'. Some English writers were no less emphatic. The Warwickshire ecclesiastic John Rous told how 'the usurper King Richard III ascended the throne of the slaughtered children'; the unknown author of the London chronicle British Library Cotton Vitellius AXVI noted that 'he also put to death the two children of King Edward, for which cause he lost the hearts of the people'; and Robert Ricart, recorder of Bristol, stated that 'in this year [i.e. the year ending 15 September 1483] the two sons of King Edward were put to silence in the Tower of London'.

Some of these writers were not as sure as they pretended to be, however, while others were clearly pursuing their own agendas. Guillaume de Rochefort was seeking to emphasise the likely consequences if the French nobility failed to unite behind their own boy king, Charles VIII; Diego de Valera mistakenly thought that Richard had killed his nephews during his brother's reign, while 'King Edward their father was waging war in Scotland'; and John Rous had prudently amended the laudatory opinion of Richard he had expressed in his *Roll* in the King's lifetime. Philippe de Commines qualified his earlier statement by suggesting elsewhere that it was Richard's principal ally, Henry Stafford, Duke of Buckingham, 'who had put the two children to death', a view also canvassed by the author of the Dutch *Divisie Chronicle*, composed about 1500, which mentions a rumour that the Princes had died of starvation (a tale told of Richard II, incidentally), adding, 'some others will say that the Duke of Buckingham killed these children hoping to become king himself'. A fragment of narrative in the Ashmolean collection (MS Ashmole 1448.60) claims that Richard killed the boys 'at the prompting of the Duke of Buckingham as it is said', while the brief chronicle edited by Richard Firth Green under the title *The Historical Notes of a London Citizen* (College of Arms MS 2M6) says that they were put to death in the Tower by Buckingham's 'vise' (that is, by his devising or on his advice).[14]

The *Great Chronicle of London*, a work probably composed by the draper Robert Fabyan, is still less certain. Fabyan noted that after Easter 1484 there was 'much whysperyng among the people that the kyng hadd put the childyr of kyng Edward to deth', but then betrays his lack of any real knowledge by suggesting that they might have been poisoned, smothered or even drowned in malmsey wine![15] Perhaps some of these writers would have quietly concurred with Thomas More's comment that the Princes' 'death and final infortune [misfortune] hathe natheles [nevertheless] so far comen in question that some remain yet in doubt whither they wer in his [Richard's] dayes destroyde or no'.[16]

The most obvious way for Richard's apologists to prove that he was not involved in the boys' murders was to search for evidence that they were still living some time after their disappearance and, preferably, had survived beyond 22 August 1485. *British Library Harleian Manuscript 433*, the record kept by Richard's clerks of the signet, refers to high-born children who were living in the King's northern household at Sheriff Hutton castle in July 1484, and also mentions a 'lord bastard' who received an allowance of clothing on 9 March 1485. The first specifies that 'my lord of Lincolne [the King's lieutenant] and my lord Morley to be at oon [one] brekefast, the Children togeder at oon brekefast [and] suche as be present of the Counsaille at oon brekefast', while the second is a warrant to Henry Davy (a tailor employed by the Great Wardrobe) 'to deliver to John Goddeslande fotemane unto the lord Bastard two dublettes of silk, oon jaket of silk, oone gowne of gloth, two shirtes and two bonetes'.[17] It would be tempting to suggest that the Princes were among the children residing at Sheriff Hutton or that the 'lord bastard' was either Edward V or Prince Richard, but nothing can be said with certainty. The executed Duke of Clarence's son and daughter together with Princess Elizabeth of York and perhaps some of Edward IV's other daughters were members of the northern household, and, while the illegitimate young lord who received the clothes could have been one of the boys in question, he could also have been John of Gloucester (or Pomfret), King Richard's own bastard son.

A second possibility, suggested by Audrey Williamson in her book *The Mystery of the Princes*, is that the boys and their mother, Queen Elizabeth Woodville, lived for a time at Sir James Tyrell's house, Gipping Hall, near Stowmarket, in Suffolk, 'by permission of the uncle', that is, Richard III.[18] It is a strange thought that the man said to have killed the boys may actually have been their protector, but it may help to explain why Elizabeth, surprisingly perhaps, came to terms with Richard about Easter 1484. Richard had alienated her by invalidating her marriage, bastardising her royal children, and executing her brother Anthony, Earl Rivers, and Richard Grey, the younger son of her first marriage. Her presence in the Westminster sanctuary (which she had entered when Richard seized power) was both a reproach to the King and an embarrassment to the Church authorities, but it is unlikely that royal and ecclesiastical pressure alone would have persuaded her to reach a settlement or that she would have succumbed to the offer of an annual pension and the promise that suitable husbands would be found for her five daughters. It could be argued that the sanctuary was becoming increasingly cramped and uncomfortable and that Elizabeth had no alternative but to deal with a man who was some fifteen years younger and who was likely to remain king for the rest of her lifetime; but she did not (presumably) have to write to her eldest son, the Marquess of Dorset, urging him to return to England and make his own peace with Richard, or offer no resistance to the King's plan to marry her eldest daughter after Queen Anne died in March 1485. She could never have forgotten what Richard had done to other members of her family, but her resentment would have been tempered by the knowledge that he had not (after all) killed her sons by King Edward and by the fact that at least one of them had been restored to her. Miss Williamson says only that the tradition, which she learned from a member of the Tyrell family, pre-dates the eighteenth century, and there is no indication of what may have become of the boys after Elizabeth was restored to her dignity as a Queen-Dowager after Bosworth. But such stories sometimes preserve a dim memory, even if they do not relate the whole truth.

Still more intriguing, ingenious even, is Jack Leslau's theory that both princes survived long into the Tudor era and lived under pseudonyms, Edward V becoming Sir Edward Guildford, son of the Comptroller of the Royal Household, and Prince Richard Dr John Clement, sometime president of the Royal College of Physicians. Clement, who married Thomas More's adopted daughter Margaret Giggs, is said to appear in a portrait of More's family painted by Hans Holbein the younger in 1527 in the guise of a young man named as 'Johanes heresius', aged 27. The figure is usually identified as More's secretary John Harris, but Leslau points out that 'Johanes heresius' could be translated as 'John the rightful heir', and suggests that the red tiger lily (which is sometimes called *Richard*-Lion-Heart) in the vase of flowers to his left may be a clue to his real identity. The portico above his head is decorated with fleur-de-lys, a symbol of royalty, and a royally purple peony (the name derives from Paion, the physician of the Gods in Greek mythology) is horizontally aligned with the top of his hat. He is, therefore, Leslau argues, both Richard, Duke of York, and Dr Clement, who, surprisingly, does not appear elsewhere in the portrait. Prince Richard would have been 54 in 1527, not 27, but Leslau points to the open door of the clock in the painting and to the decorative waxing half-moon above its face. The open door could, he suggests, imply that someone has been changing the time, and that 'Johanes heresius' is shown, like the moon, at only half his true age.[19]

Dr Clement was buried in St Rombaut's Cathedral in Mechelen (Malines) when he died in July 1571, and Mr Leslau always hoped it would be possible to compare his DNA with that of Edward IV and Elizabeth Woodville (his supposed parents), or with samples taken from the remains of his 'niece' Jane Guildford, whose grave is in Chelsea Old Church in London. Sadly, none of this had been possible when Leslau himself died in December 2004, partly, it may be surmised, because the religious authorities in the several locations were unconvinced by what one historian has called 'a brilliant flight of fancy'.[20] The problem is that it is unlikely that Thomas More (or anyone else) would have let an artist into a closely guarded state secret and encouraged him to include clues to it in his paintings; and, secondly, that Dr Clement was apparently too young to have been Richard of York. We know almost nothing of Clement's early life, but, if he was Prince Richard, he would have been 52 when he qualified as a doctor at Siena in 1525, 71 when he became president of the Royal College of Physicians in 1544, and 98 when he died in 1571. This is perhaps just possible, but it seems highly improbable that a man could have 'developed' so late in that era and then enjoyed such a remarkable old age.[21]

Another, older debate that could also be resolved by DNA technology is the identity of some bones discovered 'ten feet deep in the ground' when a staircase connecting the White Tower (of London) with an adjacent building was demolished in 1674. They were assumed to be the remains of the two Princes, because Thomas More had described how James Tyrell had buried their bodies 'at the stayre foote, metely depe in the grounde' after he had killed them; but More had also stated that 'a prieste of syr Robert Brakenbury toke up the bodyes again, and secretelye entered [interred] them in such place, as by the occasion of his deathe, whiche only knew it, could never synce come to light'.[22] There was, therefore, no reason to assume that these were the bodies of Edward V and Prince Richard (unless, of course, the priest had reburied them under another staircase!), and they were not the only remains found in the building in the Stuart period. A note added to a copy of More's *History* on 17 August 1647 recorded that, when Lord Grey and Sir Walter Raleigh were imprisoned in the Tower (that is, between 1603 and 1614), a 'little roome', 7 or 8 feet square, was discovered with the bones of two children 'supposed of 6 or 8 yeares of age' lying on a table.[23] These, too, were assumed to be the bodies of the Princes, but no efforts were made to preserve them, and they have been overshadowed by the misguided certainty that attended the discovery of 1674.

The remains found in Grey's and Raleigh's time could not have been those of Edward IV's sons if the estimates of their ages were at all accurate, but the problem is that children develop at different rates. When Professor William Wright examined the 1674 skeletons in 1933 he concluded that they were the remains of two boys, the elder aged between 12 and 13 and the younger between 9 and 11; but others have suggested that, while the elder child may have been 15 or 16, the younger need have been no more than 7 or 8. Prince Richard's child-bride, Anne Mowbray, was almost 9 when she died in 1481 but had the skeletal development of a 6-year-old; and so strong was the presumption that these were the bones of the Princes that Professor Wright did not even try to determine if they were male. They rest today in the urn in Westminster Abbey in which Charles II interred them four years after their discovery, and the Church authorities have declined to allow them to be re-examined. All we can say is that most bodies, and certainly royal bodies, would have been buried in the Tower church of St Peter ad Vincula, and, while a twenty-first-century inspection of the bones would certainly be less biased, it would not necessarily prove that they were those of the Princes or tell us who (if anyone) killed them. The fact that the remains were discovered at a depth of 10 feet could itself imply that the children concerned had died much earlier than 1483.

The identities and fates of these youngsters and those whose bones were found between 1603 and 1614 will perhaps always remain a mystery, and the same may be true of the identity (although not the fate) of another of the Tower's inmates, Perkin Warbeck. Warbeck, or Osbeck, who claimed to be Prince Richard, troubled Henry VII from when he first appeared at Cork, in Ireland, in 1491 until he was captured at Beaulieu Abbey, near Taunton, after the failure of his third invasion of England six years later. He was recognised by several European rulers when it suited them to bring pressure to bear on Henry, and James IV, King of Scots, gave him his kinswoman, Lady Katherine Gordon, in marriage; but most Englishmen either did not believe he was Edward IV's son or no longer cared. His confession, that he was the son of one John Osbeck, 'countroller of the toun of Turnay' (Tournai), and a rather impersonal letter he wrote to his natural mother asking her to send him money, may be genuine or may have been dictated to him by Henry. But he never (so far as is known) betrayed himself by an obvious blunder, and he resembled his 'father' so closely that some still argue that he really was 'King Richard IV'.[24] The main difficulty is that, although he told the Spanish Queen Isabella that 'a certain lord' who had been ordered to kill him 'having compassion on my innocence preserved me alive and in safety [and] sent me abroad with two persons who should watch over and take charge of me', he always declined to produce witnesses or name names. 'As for the manner of my escape,' he subsequently told King James, 'it is fit it should pass in silence or, at least, in a more secret relation; for that it may concern some alive and the memory of some that are dead.' This may have been true or it may have been a convenient way of avoiding the one question that everyone was bound to ask him, and equally puzzling is why

Henry declined to allow foreigners to identify him and apparently failed to confront him with his own 'sisters'. Both the French and Spanish sovereigns offered to send persons who had known either Prince Richard or Perkin to England, and Elizabeth of York, Henry's queen, would surely have recognised her own brother; but either the King knew that the young man was an impostor (and needed no further confirmation), or he genuinely feared that someone would recognise him as Richard of York. All we can say is that 'Perkin' was not accepted by most of his contemporaries, and that none of his powerful foreign friends were able to save him from being executed as a commoner in 1499.[25]

Queen Isabella and her husband, King Ferdinand, were perhaps less certain than Henry that Warbeck was an impostor,[26] and their enquiries added a curious footnote to the Princes' story. They arranged for several Portuguese worthies who had known Perkin or Prince Richard to be formally questioned at Setubal in April 1496, and were delighted with the testimony of a nobleman named Rui de Sousa, who had seen Richard while on an embassy to England in 1482. De Sousa dutifully (or prudently) stated that Warbeck did not resemble the Duke of York he remembered, and added that he had 'heard it said that they had put him and his brother too, the Prince of Wales, in a fortress where a body of water passed by, and that they bled them, and they died from the forced bleeding'.[27]

The idea that the Princes were killed accidentally by over-zealous medical attention sounds bizarre to put it mildly, but Edward V could well have been bled to cure or alleviate his illness and Prince Richard because it would do him good. Healthy people regularly subjected themselves to bloodletting because they thought it prevented the blood from stagnating in different parts of the body, and Richard could have been subjected to the same treatment as his elder brother 'just in case'. We have no way of knowing if this is indeed what happened – just as we have no way of knowing how many other thousands of medieval people were killed by the mistaken beliefs of their doctors – and in the absence of any real evidence it remains just another possibility. Richard III might have offered it as an excuse for the sudden demise of his nephews, but would anyone have believed him if he had?[28]

Curiously, no one seems to have impersonated Edward V, but Gordon Smith has suggested that he re-emerged in Ireland in 1487 in the guise of the pretender Lambert Simnel.[29] Simnel, the son of an Oxford tradesman, had been sucked into a conspiracy organised by enemies of the new Tudor dynasty and groomed to impersonate Edward, Earl of Warwick (the Yorkist heir if the two Princes had perished), who was a prisoner in the Tower of London. It is usually accepted that he was captured at Stoke Field and became a turnspit in Henry VII's kitchens; but Mr Smith suggests that the boy used to foment rebellion in Ireland was, in fact, the young King Edward, and that Simnel replaced him after he had been killed in the battle. Henry, he argues, used him to confirm his previous assertion that the boy in Ireland was an impostor, and points to Lord Bacon's comment that the pretender was aged 15 (Edward V's age in 1485–6 when Simnel was taken to Ireland), whereas the lad who became a turnspit was, according to the November Act of Attainder, only 10. It is curious that, when Sir Edward Poynings and Dr William Warham visited Margaret of Burgundy in 1493 to protest the assistance she was giving to Perkin Warbeck, Warham taxed her with having given birth to *two* princes of 180 months (that is, 15 years) of age. Margaret had supplied 'Simnel' with a force of German mercenaries, so he was clearly the first of her two 'children'; but whether this amounts to conclusive evidence that Edward V survived into Henry VII's reign is quite another matter. The youth in Ireland was apparently plausible enough to satisfy a herald whom Henry sent to question him, but there must have been many both there and in northern England who would have been aware that the lad kept at court and treated derisively was not the young man they had known as King Edward. It would have been almost impossible to substitute one for the other and maintain the pretence against all comers; and more evidence is needed before the youth crowned in Dublin can be regarded as other than a 'feigned boy'.[30]

So far, all the information we have considered has been conventional, but there is another, more controversial, source that must be included in any impartial survey of the problem. In 1996 the Reverend John Dening, a retired Anglican priest, published a book entitled *Secret History: The Truth about Richard III and the Princes*, in which he described a series of contacts with King Richard (and also with Edward IV) effected through the medium Bryan Gibson. 'Richard' told Dening that the Princes had indeed been smothered in the Tower before being buried in a forest, but maintained that this had never been his intention. He had, admittedly, signed a document formally deposing Edward V, but others had then decided that deposition also meant elimination. Who were these 'others'? No names were given, but the Church in general, and one bishop or cardinal in particular, were held to be the real culprits. Dening assumed that this was John Morton, who might, possibly, have talked his gaoler Buckingham into killing the boys on either his own behalf or Henry Tudor's; but there is no real evidence that Morton could (or would) have killed Edward IV's sons.[31] Morton was a small man, not the 'rather largish gentleman in church-robes' seen by Gibson,[32] and there is nothing in the record of these meetings that ties in with any previously unsuspected or corroborative evidence. We are told that Edward IV was 'helped over' to the other side while Henry VI 'created his own passing', but the allegations are again too unspecific for us to say whether or not they might be true.[33]

What is clear, however, even from this brief survey, is that there are almost as many theories as there are theorists, and that, while some of them could live side by side with others, the rest are mutually contradictory. The Princes may have been killed, although by whom or on whose orders is uncertain, or they may have survived in one of several different guises. Edward V could have become Edward Guildford or Lambert Simnel, although both suggestions are highly speculative: Prince Richard's personas of Dr Clement and Perkin Warbeck are more plausible, but he could not have been both of them and may not have been either. Curiously, however, when Polydore Vergil revised the 1512–13 manuscript of his *Anglica Historia* before its publication at Basle in 1534, he mentioned a rumour that the boys had 'migrated secretly to some other country'.[34] This was entirely contrary to the official line that they had been murdered and may be no more than an echo of the claims made by Warbeck; but why bother to notice the story after half a century unless there was at least a slight possibility that it could be accurate? Vergil may have felt that the 'threat' the Princes posed to the Tudors was now so minimal that he could indulge in a little speculation; but was he again hinting that there was perhaps more to the mystery without actually contradicting what he had written earlier? Lord Bacon remarked in the next century that at 'this time' (he was referring to the events of 1487) 'it was still whispered every where that at least one of the children [i.e. sons] of Edward IV was living'. He could have added that such stories were complete nonsense, but said only that King Henry was not by nature inclined 'to disperse these mists'.[35] The general consensus was that one of the Princes *could have*, we might even say possibly *had*, survived whatever might have happened in the Tower of London, even if none of the theories offered a convincing or even satisfactory explanation. It is this explanation that the following chapters will seek to provide.

# TWO

## *Richard of Eastwell*

E astwell, with its lakeside manor house and church, is one
of Kent's best-kept secrets. It is an ancient place – with a
collection of stories to match its antiquity[1] – and a haven of
tranquillity far removed from the bustle of Ashford only 3½
miles distant. There has been much change over the centuries –
the lake was formed only in the mid-nineteenth century, the
great house on the opposite side of the park is now a hotel, and
the church stands in ruins – but the trees still gaze down on the
spring lambs as they have for generations and there is a sense of
timelessness, of being part of a scene that could belong to
almost any era. Visitors to the park now walk along part of the
modern North Downs Way instead of the pathways trod by
their forebears, but there are still corners that a medieval or
Tudor villager would find familiar were he to return today.

Eastwell belonged in late Saxon times to a thegn called
Frederic, but it became part of Bishop Odo of Bayeux's earldom
of Kent after the Conquest and was granted to Hugh (Hugo) de
Montfort, a Norman knight.[2] The Montforts held the manor
for three generations, after which it was given to the de Criol
family, and then passed by marriage to the Lords Poynings,

19

who distinguished themselves in the Hundred Years War.[3] Robert, the fourth baron, died in 1446 leaving his property to his granddaughter Eleanor, *de jure suo jure* Baroness Poynings, who had married Henry Percy, third Earl of Northumberland, nine years earlier. Northumberland supported the House of Lancaster in the Wars of the Roses and lost both his life and his estates at Towton, but the lands were restored to his son, another Henry, in 1470. It is this Henry, the fourth earl, who is remembered principally for his inactivity at the battle of Bosworth and who was slain by his fellow northerners while trying to collect Henry VII's taxes in 1489.

The Percies held Eastwell manor until the sixth earl of Northumberland died childless in 1537, when it was bought by three daughters and co-heiresses of Sir Christopher Hales, a trusted royal servant who had served Henry VIII as solicitor-general, attorney-general and master of the rolls. They may have intended to live there when they could dislodge the sitting tenant Sir Thomas Moyle, another prominent lawyer; but Moyle declined to vacate while he was involved in the great business of the suppression of the monasteries and eventually bought the estate from them. The Moyles had occupied the old manor house (now 'Lake House') for nearly a century – Sir Walter Moyle, Sir Thomas's grandfather, had probably leased it from the Earl of Northumberland when he moved to Kent in the 1440s – and it is instructive that, although Sir Thomas could not, apparently, afford to buy the property in 1537 (at the beginning of the Dissolution), he was able to acquire it *after* the greater monasteries had been ransacked a few years later. He built a new mansion about half a mile to the east-north-east of Lake House, and bequeathed it to his elder daughter, Katherine, and her husband, Sir Thomas Finch, when he died in 1560. Their son, Sir Moyle Finch, was given licence to crenellate in 1589, and the estate passed on his death to his wife, Elizabeth, who was subsequently created Viscountess Maidstone and Countess of Winchilsea in her own right.

Elizabeth, who died in 1633, was the ancestress of the ten individuals who held Eastwell and the title Earl of Winchilsea for the next 260 years. We need notice only two of them: Heneage Finch, the fifth earl, whose antiquarian interests inspired much of what follows; and George William Finch-Hatton, the tenth earl, who once fought a duel with the Duke of Wellington and whose father had employed the Italian architect Joseph Bonomi to redesign and rebuild the great house around the turn of the nineteenth century. The eleventh and last earl leased the property to Prince Alfred, Duke of Edinburgh (second son of Queen Victoria), in 1874, and it became a royal residence until the Duke and his family moved to Malta twelve years later. It was sold to Lord Gerard in 1893, and had a number of other distinguished owners and tenants, including Sir John de Fonblanqua Pennefather, baronet, who again remodelled the house in 1926. The estate was bought by the Countess Midleton four years later, and was managed by her son, Captain George Brodrick, until her death in 1977. It was then sold to Thomas Bates and Sons of Essex, whose family developed the mansion as a hotel before selling to a conglomerate, which kept the house and some land but disposed of the rest to a local farmer. The hotel business was acquired by its present owners in 1993.

The church, dedicated to St Mary, was begun about 1380 and built in the Decorated and Perpendicular styles. Charles Igglesden tells us that it boasted six bells (one ancient and five presented by the tenth Earl of Winchilsea in 1842), and that the great west window had been made from 'a collection of ancient glass, gathered from many places of note' by the Earl's father. Some of the fragments had been placed upside down, making them heraldically inaccurate, but among the royal coats of arms were two of Queen Elizabeth's, one dated 1570. Edward IV's 'sun in splendour' and Henry VII's 'crown in a thorn bush' were also represented, and there were parts of shields of the Poynings family together with coats of arms that John Kemp (who came from nearby Wye) would have borne when he was Bishop of London (1421–5) and Archbishop of Canterbury (1452–4). Three helmets that had belonged to members of the Finch family hung on the walls, and particularly noteworthy were the 'beautifully carved chancel screen and the pew poppy-heads'. 'Every panel in the former is delicately worked to a design different from the others,' wrote Igglesden, 'while none of the numerous poppy-heads are alike.'[4] The pew occupied by the Finch-Hatton family was decorated with a rebus displaying a small bird (Finch), with a hat and a tun (or cask) beneath.

St Mary's was kept in good repair until the Second World War, although what happened then is a little uncertain. Alison Weir says that it was damaged by a V2, a long-range rocket used by the Germans, but Philip Dormer blames local British troops, whose 'blasting, during training operations, caused plaster to fall and doors to burst open through pressure waves'.[5] The real culprit may have been the chalk blocks which had been used to construct much of the interior, and which weakened as they absorbed water from the nearby lake. Early in February 1951 a workman repairing the road near the church during a gale heard a loud rumbling noise, and saw the roof collapse into the rest of the structure. Rebuilding was not an option – the parish was small and there were several churches of greater architectural interest in the immediate vicinity – and only the tower, the west wall and a small chapel in the south-western corner were left standing when the nave and chancel were dismantled in 1958. The site was cleared of rubbish with the help of parishioners and other friends of the building (see Appendix 2), and has been under the care of the 'Friends of Friendless Churches' since 1980. They and English Heritage have helped to preserve much of what we see today.

The collapse of the roof inevitably damaged parts of the interior, but some of the more valuable contents were fortunately unharmed. The bells were sold in 1952 (for around £450, according to Philip Dormer), the ancient glass was sent to King's College, Cambridge, and other places, and the monuments, after spending some years in a purpose-built brick shelter, found a home in the Victoria and Albert Museum in 1968. These included the ornate tomb chest of Sir Thomas Moyle and his wife, Katherine, the reclining figure of Emily Georgina, second wife of the tenth earl, known as the 'White Lady',[6] and the effigies of Sir Moyle Finch and Elizabeth, Countess of Winchilsea, finely carved in Carrara marble. Sir Moyle's eyes are closed, but those of his wife are open, suggesting that the work was at least begun in her lifetime. It once boasted eight columns of black marble supporting an ornate canopy, but these were removed as long ago as 1756.

Lake House, which has withstood the ravages of time rather better than St Mary's, has been described as being of 'exceptional interest'. It is a typical small manor house measuring 45ft by 26ft 6in, built in the Norman style by John de Criol about the year 1300. Hasted's *History of Kent* (1799) refers to it as the 'court lodge', indicating that this was where the Leet Court, which dealt with estate matters, was held before the lord or his steward. Its flint rubble walls, 2½ft thick, are pierced by four Early English windows (now blocked), and retain some of the original stone quoins. Lack of adequate foundations caused the roof to push the walls outwards, and this explains why parts of the structure had to be reinforced with massive brick buttresses and perhaps why the roof had to be rebuilt in the seventeenth century. Inside, the first-floor Norman hall and ground-level undercroft have been partitioned and 'improved' by the addition of fireplaces and chimneys. The latter were clearly in place by the Jacobean period, since the remaining older roof timbers are blackened by smoke from the open hearth (probably a 'pedestal' hearth built up 7ft from ground level so as to be flush with the hall floor), which once heated the building. Stout and enduring, it was at one time empty and semi-derelict, but is now happily a home once again.[7]

One day in 1542 or 1543, an elderly but plainly still active man arrived in Eastwell and made his way to Lake House. He had come, he said, because he had heard that Sir Thomas Moyle was looking for skilled bricklayers to help build his new mansion, and he was willing to offer him his services. Sir Thomas's overseer thought him well spoken if somewhat taciturn, and engaged him after making the usual enquiries about his experience and recent employment. The newcomer, who gave his name as Richard, seemed to prefer his own company to that of the other, generally younger, workmen, but it was how he spent his leisure time that gave rise to comment and brought him to Sir Thomas's attention when he strolled over from the old house to monitor progress. This was an age in which literacy was still confined to the upper classes, yet Richard could read Latin and enjoyed nothing better that to sit apart with a book when he had the opportunity. The implication was clearly that he and his family had once been more than bricklayers, and Sir Thomas was intrigued to discover how and why a gentleman (as he supposed) had turned to 'trade' to earn his keep.

We owe this report, what happened next and the 'solution' to the mystery to a letter written by Dr Thomas Brett, a non-juring clergyman who lived at Spring Grove, near Wye, to his friend William Warren, President of Trinity Hall, Cambridge, on 1 September 1733. Brett had resigned his livings of Betteshanger and Ruckinge on George I's accession because his conscience would not allow him to take the oaths imposed by the government, but he remained on good terms with the Finch family and sometimes called on them at Eastwell Park. The good

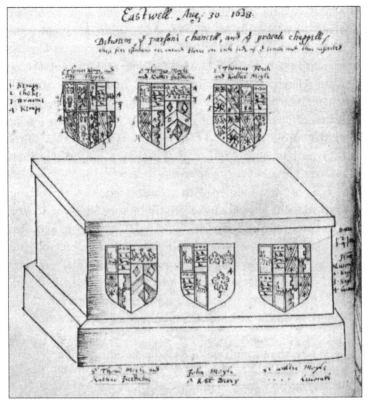

Monument to Sir Thomas and Lady Moyle, drawn in 1628.

doctor recalled how, some thirteen years earlier (that is, about Michaelmas 1720), the then Earl of Winchilsea had told him of a tradition concerning Richard which had been handed down in his family and which his lordship apparently had no reason to question. 'When Sir Thomas Moyle built that house (that is Eastwell Place),' wrote Brett paraphrasing Winchilsea,

he observed his chief bricklayer, whenever he left off work, retired with a book. Sir Thomas had a curiosity to know, what book the man read; but it was some time before he could discover it: he still putting the book up if any one came toward him. However, at last, Sir Thomas surprized him, & snatched the book from him; & looking into it, found it to be Latin. Hereupon he examined him, & finding he pretty well understood that language, he enquired, how he came by his learning? Hereupon the man told him, as he had been a good master to him, he would venture to trust him with a secret that he had never before revealed to any one. He then informed him.

That he was boarded with a Latin schoolmaster, without knowing who his parents were, 'till he was fifteen or sixteen years old; only a gentleman (who took occasion to acquaint him he was no relation to him) came once a quarter, & paid for his board, and took care to see that he wanted nothing. And one day, this gentleman took him & carried him to a fine, great house, where he passed through several stately rooms, in one of which he left him, bidding him stay there.

Then a man finely drest, with a star and garter, came to him; asked him some questions; talked kindly to him; & gave him some money. Then the 'forementioned gentleman returned, and conducted him back to his school.

Some time after the same gentleman came to him again, with a horse & proper accoutrements, & told him, he must make a journey with him into the country. They went into Leicestershire, & came to Bosworth Field; & he was carried to K. Richard III. tent. The King embraced him, & told him he was his son. But, child, says he, tomorrow I must fight for my crown. And, assure your self, if I lose that, I will lose my life too: but I hope to preserve both. Do you stand in such a place (directing him to a particular place) where you may see the battle, out of danger. And, when I have gained the victory, come to me; I will then own you to be mine, & take care of you. But, if I should be so unfortunate to lose the battel, then shift as well as you can, & take care to let nobody know that I am your father; for no mercy will be shewed to any one so [nearly] related to me. Then the king gave him a purse of gold, & dismissed him.

He followed the king's directions. And, when he saw the battel was lost & the king killed, he hasted to London; sold his horse, & fine cloaths; &, the better to conceal himself from all suspicion of being son to a king, & that he might have means to live by his honest labour, he put himself apprentice to a bricklayer. But, having a competent skill in the Latin tongue, he was unwilling to lose it; and having an inclination also to reading, & no delight in the conversation of those he was obliged to work with, he generally spent all the time he had to spare in reading by himself.

Sir Thomas said, you are now old, and almost past your labour; I will give you the running of my kitchen as long as you live. He answered, Sir, you have a numerous family; I have been used to live retired; give me leave to build a house of one room for myself in such a field, & there, with your good leave, I will live & die: and, if you have any work I can do for you, I shall be ready to serve you. Sir Thomas granted his request, he built his house, and there continued to his death.[8]

Sir Thomas seems to have accepted the story, although whether he believed it or merely humoured the old man is uncertain. Richard could have sensed an opportunity to turn Moyle's interest to his own advantage and made the tale up on the spur of the moment, but his reward, a peaceful and secure retirement, owed more to his good service than his account of his life's history. No drawing or word-picture of the mansion they both worked to build has come down to us, but it presumably continued the fashion of constructing fortified manor houses of red brick begun in the previous century. The decoration of the walls and towers with patterns worked in contrasting blue brick (as, for example, at St John's College, Cambridge, and at the bishop's palace at Ely) was a skilled task that would be appropriately rewarded, and, if Richard was the master or chief bricklayer (as Brett suggests he was), his status and remuneration would have matched that of the master mason (who doubled as the architect) and the master carpenter.[9] He was certainly experienced enough to occupy this position, and, although we imagined him coming to Eastwell to offer his services, it is also possible that he had been 'head-hunted' because his abilities were well known in the area. A master-craftsman then, whose skills commanded the respect of his colleagues, even if they thought him aloof and a little strange.

The Earl of Winchilsea was also the source for a second, slightly different, version of the story, which appeared in an anonymous work entitled *The Parallel: or a Collection of Extraordinary Cases Relating to Concealed Births and Disputed Successions* published in 1744. This says that in 1469 Richard, Duke of Gloucester, 'had an amour, or for aught I know contracted a private marriage with some lady of quality . . . and towards the latter end of the same year this lady brought him a son'. The boy Richard spent the first seven years of his life being cared for by a nurse (whom he assumed was his mother) in a country village, and it was only after this that his education was entrusted to a Latin schoolmaster who resided in or near Lutterworth in Leicestershire. He developed a particular liking for the works of Horace, and was engrossed in reading one of them when Sir Thomas Moyle surprised him at Eastwell over half a century later. The rest is very similar to Dr Brett's story, although Brett describes the matter in rather fewer words.

What, then, are we to make of this 'Richard of Eastwell' and what some would consider his rather improbable biography? The one certainty is that a man who, by the end of his life, was known as Richard Plantagenet lived for a time in the village and died there on 22 December 1550. His death is recorded in

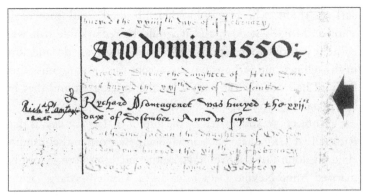

Highlighted copy of the entry in the Eastwell parish register, AD 1550. 'Rychard Plantagenet was buryed the xxij's daye of Desember. Anno ut supra', with a mark in the left margin said to signify that the deceased was of noble birth.

the parish register, and, although it is a copy of the original entry (made, probably, by Josias Nichols, the then rector, on 9 October 1598), there is no reason to think it a forgery. R.H. D'Elboux has commented that 'the entries of 1538–1598 are a transcript . . . and may well have been in Latin; if so one may hazard that Plantagenet was a pedantic translation of Broom, and with the conjecture dismiss the romantic offspring of the White Boar'. But there is no evidence that the surviving register has been translated from the Latin, and the suggestion must be regarded as somewhat perverse. Similarly, it has been claimed that a mark next to the entry indicates that Richard was known to be of noble or royal blood; but this story was started in 1767 by Philip Parsons, the then rector of Eastwell, and the truth of the matter is apparently that one of the Finches placed marks against some names that were of interest to him with the intention of copying them out.[10] The story depends on the tradition handed down in the Moyle and Finch families; but the fifth Earl of Winchilsea could have heard it from the third earl (d. 1689), whose grandmother, Elizabeth, had known Sir Thomas Moyle's widow, and it would be remarkable if it was entirely without foundation. Such stories always gain and lose in the telling; but perhaps we can accept the basic premiss that Richard had not always been a humble bricklayer, and that he had a 'past' he preferred to conceal.

One objection, anticipated by the author of *The Parallel*, is that Richard of Gloucester acknowledged two other illegitimate children, John ('of Pomfret') and Katherine, both born before he married Anne Neville in or after 1472. Contemporary society regarded such children as the inevitable consequence of human frailty 'from whiche healthe of bodye, in great prosperitye and fortune, wythoute a specyall grace hardelye refrayneth',[11] as Thomas More has it; and since Gloucester was never, so far as we know, taken to task for having sired John and Katherine, it is difficult to explain why he should be so coy about 'Richard'. The writer suggests that this was because the year of his birth, 1469–70, was a time of great trouble for the Yorkists – Edward IV was held prisoner by Warwick the Kingmaker for some weeks and then subsequently driven into exile along with his younger brother – but if Gloucester concealed his infant son to protect him in the short term he could still have owned him after Edward recovered his kingdom in 1471. He allegedly thought little about him after Edward, his legitimate son, was born in 1475 or 1476; and it was only Edward's death eight or nine years later that, the author suggests, caused Gloucester (who had now become King Richard III) to have young Richard brought to him for their first interview. Queen Anne's death in March 1485 removed the last remaining obstacle to his revealing his affair with the boy's mother, and only the verdict of Bosworth prevented Richard 'Plantagenet' from being publicly acknowledged as the King's son.

It almost goes without saying that, if Queen Anne knew of the existence of John and Katherine, she would not have been particularly scandalised by the revelation that her husband had a third such child, and the secrecy that surrounded 'Richard' cannot be explained in these terms. It is also most unlikely that a boy who was placed in the care of a schoolmaster when he was 7 would still be living with the same schoolmaster (and, presumably, still learning his lessons) when he was 15 or 16. Children were typically sent away from home when they were 7 or 8 (to develop self-reliance and to make useful contacts rather than to prevent their parents from becoming too fond of them in case they died early), but maturity came quickly and they entered the adult world in their early teens. Not all of them could, or would, wish to emulate Henry Percy (Hotspur), who was commanding troops when he was only 12; but Richard of Gloucester's own formal tutelage had ended at this age, and John of Pomfret, young Richard's half-brother, cannot have been much older when his father named him Captain of Calais in September 1483.[12] Richard had also reached an age when he could perform useful service, and would almost certainly have been trained for whatever role Gloucester had in mind for him long before he reached 15 or 16. The implication is that he had not yet embarked on such training and was therefore several years younger than he claimed to be.

So far so good, but could a youth who was perhaps only 11 or 12 have made his own way to London and decided to apprentice himself to a bricklayer? It seems remarkable that, having been brought to his father at Bosworth, he should have been left entirely alone in the world thereafter, and one wonders what became of the unnamed gentleman who had escorted him and paid his board. He could have been killed in the battle, of course, but it is perhaps more likely that he was only one of several of the late King's followers charged with the task of escorting Richard from the area before any harm could come to him. We may assume that their instructions were to take him to a place of safety before shifting for themselves (whether by soliciting pardons or fomenting conspiracies against the new government), and that they would have entrusted his longer-term future to someone who enjoyed their confidence and who could receive a young stranger without arousing suspicion. Richard may not have told Sir Thomas Moyle everything, of course, and perhaps said he had gone to London (where he would have been almost as anonymous as a modern Londoner), to avoid explaining where, and with whom, he had been living for many of the intervening years.

Dr Warren, the recipient of Brett's letter, gave it with the latter's permission to Francis Peck, the antiquary, who published it in the second volume of his *Desiderata Curiosa* in 1779. Peck also refers to 'another account' of Richard's story that had come to his notice, and gives in the first person what he says are 'the most material differences' between this and Brett's narrative. Unfortunately some of his interpolations – for example, that the man who wore the star and garter 'felt my limbs and joints' and that Sir Thomas Moyle was able to inspect Richard's book while he was asleep – do not add much to what we know already, and all of them must be treated with caution. The statement that 'I was brought up at my nurse's house (whom I took for my mother) 'till I was seven years old . . . then a gentleman, whom I did not know, took me from thence, and carried me to a private school in Leicestershire' has probably been borrowed from the *Parallel*, and there is no reason to suppose the anonymous author had real evidence to support his assertion that King Richard chose not to reveal his identity (and did not tell the boy that he was his father) at their second meeting before Bosworth.

He [the King] asked me, whether we heard any news at our school? I said, the news was, that the Earl of Richmond was landed, & marched against K. Richard. He said, he was on the king's side, & a friend to Richard . . . & said, if K. Richard gets the better in the contest, you may then come to court, & you shall be provided for. But if he is worsted or killed, take this money, and go to London, & provide for yourself as well as you can.

Richard did not know how to reach London, but in this version of the story was told first to make his way to Leicester, where, he says:

I saw a dead body brought to town upon an horse. And, upon looking stedfastly upon it, I found it to be my father. I then went forward to town [London]. And (my genius leading me to architecture) as I was looking on a fine house which was building there, one of the workmen employed me about something, &, finding me very handy, took me to his house, & taught me the trade, which now occupies me.[13]

It would appear that he had by now put two and two together and realised that he was the King's son, but the whole scenario lacks conviction. He would surely not have risked mingling with the Tudor army in Leicester when he had been urged to escape as quickly as possible, and there is the same (improbable) assumption that his future was left to chance rather than entrusted to one or more of his father's adherents. No writer explains why, if he found himself alone and friendless, he did not simply travel the few miles to Lutterworth and the safety of his old school and teacher, or why he did not take both himself and his new wealth to the court of his 'aunt', Duchess Margaret, in Burgundy. We are informed that his father gave him ten pieces of gold '*viz.* crown-gold, which was the current money then, and worth ten shillings apiece' at their first meeting in the great house, and the large sum of 1,200 such pieces before Bosworth. This (£600) would not have disgraced the annual income of a minor baron, but there is no mention of where Richard kept it, or how much he spent before he began to earn his keep.

Richard's name has been associated with a number of buildings and structures that stand, or used to stand, in the park at Eastwell, and the Earl of Winchilsea told Dr Brett that he remembered seeing a small dwelling called Plantagenet's Cottage in his youth. It had been demolished by his father, the third earl (much to his disgust, apparently, since he told Brett that 'I would as soon have pulled down this house' (the new manor); but he did not doubt that it was the one-roomed lodge that the old man had built with Sir Thomas Moyle's permission and that it confirmed at least this part of his story. A house in the park is still known as Plantagenet's Cottage, and had a castellated pseudo-Gothic façade when Charles Igglesden noticed it in the course of preparing the third volume of his *A Saunter through Kent with Pen and Pencil*, published in 1901. Igglesden says that it is

> no doubt very ancient, for its walls, which are of burnt earth and ballast, are about eighteen inches thick. The windows are of the shape peculiar to all the cottages on the estate, and the front door inside the massive porch is of oak between two and three inches thick, coffer-panelled and studded with large-headed nails. The porch is very remarkable, being built of solid brickwork and carried up high above the roof. In the summer time it is covered with Virginia creeper, but with the falling leaf a dummy window is visible. There is an almost square cellar beneath one of the rooms, and this is credited with having been the hiding place of Plantagenet in times of necessity.[14]

The property has been remodelled since Igglesden's time, and looks very different today.

The cottage may stand on the site of Richard's original construction, but Igglesden also mentions a curious building known as Little Jack's House, which he says used to stand near the reservoir.

The house now called 'Plantagenet's Cottage'. Pen and ink drawing on a postcard by Saxon Barton (founder, Richard III Society).

It was a brick building of two rooms, one on top of the other. Each contained a fireplace, but nothing is known for what purpose it was used beyond the statement that it was utilised for the isolation of a horse suffering from glanders. Until it became too ruinous for use buck beans were stored in it. There is a local tradition that the Plantagenet outcast hid there, but no conclusive evidence can be gleaned.[15]

The idea that Richard felt threatened during his time at Eastwell and sometimes had occasion to conceal himself is probably no more that later, largely idle, speculation, and the same may be true of two other features associated with him, what is still called 'Plantagenet's well' and his supposed monument, which stands in the ruins of the church. The well lies 'within a stone's throw' of the cottage, says Igglesden, 'near the gas works on the Boughton road'.

It is between twenty and thirty feet deep and for a long time was a receptacle for all kinds of rubbish. It was an object of interest until about six years ago [i.e. the mid-1890s] when it was filled up with building refuse and thereby closed. A railing now cuts off that part of the park, but two fine trees standing close together mark the historic spot.[16]

The well is now bricked round for safety, but it is still possible to visit the much-damaged tomb and to visualise it as Igglesden saw it at about the turn of the nineteenth century.

Against the north wall, within the communion rails, is an ancient monument of Bethersden marble, which, tradition says, denotes the burial place of Sir Richard Plantagenet. The fact that the tomb originally had two brasses and a supplicatory prayer such as 'Jesu, Mercy', or 'Mary, Help', repeated four times on scrolls at the corners, leads archaeologists of the present day to confidently declare that the tomb is not that of Plantagenet, while additional doubt is cast on the tradition by the surmise that Sir Thomas Moyle, who held high State offices, including that of Speaker in the House of Commons, would not risk incurring Royal displeasure by erecting such a monument to the son of a king whose identity he had helped to hide.[17]

This view is confirmed by R.H. D'Elboux, who saw the tomb in, or shortly before, 1946 and described it as follows.

Half under a recessed arch in the north wall of the chancel is an altar tomb of Bethersden marble, the slab of which, though very worn, still retains traces of the indents for brasses. It measures 23 by 53 inches, and has a projection from the wall of 10¼ inches, with a chamfer edge of 2¼ inches on three sides, once containing a brass inscription an inch wide. The sides of the tomb are plain surfaced.

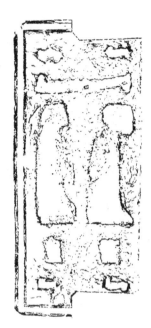

Sketch of 'Richard Plantagenet's tomb',
*c.* 1946, showing traces of indents for brasses
(from *Archaeologia Cantiana*, 59 (1946)).

On the slab there have been four brass scrolls, one at each
corner, and then one long lateral one immediately above the
figures. The sinister figure was certainly that of a female of
*c.* 1480–90, with the late type of butterfly headdress and
probably wearing a mantle; the dexter is the most worn of
the indents, and at first glance seems also to represent a
female, but is more likely a male with long hair in civilian or
judicial garb. The sinister longitudinal edge of this figure's
indent is completely obliterated. Both figures faced to the
dexter, towards the altar. Below the dexter figure was a group
of sons, seemingly two, and below the female a larger group
of daughters.[18]

The figures cannot be identified with certainty but most
probably represent Sir Walter Moyle, his wife Margaret,

daughter and co-heiress of John Luccomb of Stevenstone, Devon, and their children. Moyle was a lawyer who was regularly summoned to Parliament and who served Edward IV as a member of various commissions and inquiries relating principally to the southern and western counties. He acted as judge of the Common bench at Queen Elizabeth Woodville's coronation on 26 May 1465 and was then knighted, but his age (he was born in 1405) may have allowed him to avoid direct, personal involvement in the Wars of the Roses. He died in or about 1480, having fathered two sons, John (Sir Thomas's father) and Richard, and possibly three daughters which would agree with the numbers apparently represented on the grave slab. He is certainly a more likely candidate than Richard Plantagenet, who, as far as we know, was unmarried and childless, and who did not arrive in Eastwell until more than sixty years after Sir Walter's death.[19]

Exposure to the elements continues to erode what remains of the structure, which is now further threatened by several sturdy young saplings growing near to its base. Ivy and moss have all but obscured any remaining traces of the indents, and even the modern plaque bearing the legend 'Reputed to be the Tomb of Richard Plantagenet 22 December 1550' is barely legible. The tradition did not, presumably, exist in the early eighteenth century, or the Earl of Winchilsea and Dr Brett would surely have mentioned it. Indeed, Brett actually remarks that 'we cannot say whether he was buried in the church or churchyard; nor is there now any other memorial of him, except the tradition in the family, & some little marks of the place where his house stood'.[20] It was probably first said to have been Richard's grave in the later eighteenth century, 'though always, by writers of discrimination, with a reservation that the monument seemed of earlier date'.[21]

This then, is all we know of Richard of Eastwell. What of his 'contemporary', Prince Richard of York?

# THREE

## *Richard of York*

Prince Richard, second son and fifth surviving child of King Edward IV and his queen, Elizabeth Woodville, was born at Shrewsbury, probably on 17 August 1473. He was fortunate to be a prince, since his father had only become king by seizing the throne in the course of the internecine struggle known as the Wars of the Roses twelve years earlier, a throne he had lost and then recovered within the space of seven months in 1470–1. The Wars are sometimes portrayed as a power struggle between two rival branches of the royal family; but they had begun as an attempt by competing noble factions to dominate the weak King Henry VI to their own advantage. Richard, Duke of York, King Edward's father, found himself excluded from the royal counsels by the dominance of his enemies, the Duke of Somerset and Henry's wife, Queen Margaret, and on two occasions in the early and mid-1450s – at Dartford in 1452 and again at St Albans in 1455 – tried to wrest power from them while protesting that he was still Henry's loyal subject. His problem was that the concept of loyal opposition did not exist in the Middle Ages, and resistance to the reigning king's will was treasonable, even if that will was being manipulated, or controlled, by others.

The Duke of York and his two principal associates, his brother-in-law Richard Neville, Earl of Salisbury, and Salisbury's son Richard, Earl of Warwick, may have been piqued by their enemies' hold over the royal government, but this was by no means their only worry. They needed access to Henry to obtain a share in the royal patronage for their retainers and well-wishers (many would not long serve a lord who could not secure these offices and annuities for them), and there was little likelihood that York would recover monies he had spent trying to bolster the English war effort in France in the 1440s from the impoverished Exchequer unless he enjoyed the King's 'ear'. Henry suffered a severe mental collapse at the beginning of August 1453, and York, his nearest adult male relative, was appointed protector; but the old favourites were restored when the King recovered, and the birth of a son to Queen Margaret in October 1453 meant that there was now little hope of change in the foreseeable future. A formal reconciliation – the so-called Love Day of 25 March 1458 – came to nothing, and the next year the Yorkist Lords were driven into exile in Ireland and Calais. Salisbury, Warwick and York's son, Edward, Earl of March, returned to England in June 1460, defeated the King at the battle of Northampton (10 July) and again subjected him to their authority; but their protestations that they meant only to reform Henry's government were made to appear fraudulent when York returned from Ireland in October and claimed that the Crown rightfully belonged to him!

The thrust of the Duke's argument was that he was descended from an elder son of Edward III than his rival, but took no account of the fact that Henry was a crowned and anointed sovereign who had already reigned for thirty-eight years. An uneasy compromise was reached whereby Henry would remain king for the rest of his life but would then be succeeded by York and his heirs instead of his own son Prince

Edward; but Queen Margaret had no intention of allowing her only child to be disinherited, and the 'agreement' led only to renewed conflict. York was killed at Wakefield on 30 December 1460 (Salisbury was executed afterwards), and Margaret defeated Warwick and regained possession of her hapless husband at the second battle of St Albans fought on 17 February 1461. The Yorkist position was now desperate, but young Edward of March, who had defeated the Welsh Lancastrians at Mortimer's Cross on 2 February, pressed on to London and was proclaimed king by Warwick and his other supporters. A dramatic and bloody victory over the royal forces at Towton, in Yorkshire, on Palm Sunday left Henry a fugitive with his cause in ruins, and confirmed that England would now be governed by Edward IV.

The new king was a tall, good-looking 19-year-old whose accession seemed to presage a new era, but contemporaries were shocked when they learned that he had married Elizabeth Woodville, the daughter of one former Lancastrian and widow of another, in May 1464. The idea of a king, or king-in-waiting, marrying a commoner for love has only recently become acceptable, and Edward's friends expected him to choose a foreign princess whose connections and dowry would benefit his country both diplomatically and financially. He tried to avoid the inevitable furore by keeping the wedding a secret; but when, in September, Warwick informed him that he had arranged a match with Bona of Savoy, the King of France's sister-in-law, he was forced to admit that he was married already. The Earl must have been deeply wounded by the fact that Edward had failed to consult him on such an important matter; but a king was not obliged to seek the advice of his nobility or to wed openly, and Warwick and others had no alternative but to accept Elizabeth as their queen.

Warwick and his friends would doubtless have recovered from the shock and the implied snub to their dignity if this had been all there was to it; but Elizabeth brought with her no fewer than five brothers and seven sisters, who all had to be given appropriate status. The sisters were married into some of the greatest noble families (to the disappointment of those who had hoped to secure the matches for their own offspring), while some of the brothers and the elder son of Elizabeth's first marriage received offices and became prominent courtiers. Warwick found it hard to accept that a family that had fought for Lancaster while he had dedicated himself to the Yorkist cause should now rival him in Edward's affections, and in 1469 inspired an uprising known as Robin of Redesdale's rebellion, which led to the defeat of the royal forces at Edgecote, near Banbury. He imprisoned Edward in Middleham castle after executing several members of the Queen's family and marrying his elder daughter to George, Duke of Clarence, the King's brother; but when it became apparent that he could not rule through Edward (because few, if any, would obey orders that clearly emanated from the Earl personally), he bowed to the inevitable and set him free.

King Edward for his part was prepared to forgive Warwick's outrageous behaviour and let bygones be bygones, but he would not allow the Earl to dictate either his policies or his choice of companions. The result was that Warwick, finding that nothing had changed, prompted a new outbreak of violence in Lincolnshire in March 1470 from which, he supposed, he would again 'rescue' his grateful master. But it was the royal forces, commanded by Edward personally, who triumphed at the battle of Empingham (Lose-cote Field), and, when Warwick was summoned to court to explain himself, he fled to France, taking Clarence, now his partner in crime, with him. The arrival of two such senior, disaffected, Yorkists presented Louis XI, 'the spider king', with a golden opportunity to spin webs around his brother of England, and at Angers on 22 July 1470 Warwick was formally reconciled with his arch-enemy Queen Margaret. It was agreed that the Earl would invade England on behalf of the House of Lancaster and restore King Henry (who had been a prisoner in the Tower since his capture in 1464), and that his reward would be the marriage of his younger daughter with Margaret's son Prince Edward, the Lancastrian heir to the throne. Warwick and Clarence returned to the West Country with a force of exiles on 13 September and King Edward moved to intercept them; but the defection of John, Marquess Montagu, Warwick's hitherto loyal brother, to the invaders proved decisive, and Edward sought refuge in Holland with a few loyal friends.

Queen Elizabeth may have considered securing the Tower against Warwick and his cronies to help resist their invasion, but when word of her husband's flight reached her she entered the Westminster sanctuary, where Edward, their first son, was born on 2 November. She was already the mother of three daughters, Elizabeth (born 1466), Mary (born 1467) and Cecily (born 1469), and in this and in other ways had faced down those who had criticised her suitability to be Edward's consort. Her few surviving letters show her taking a firm, no-nonsense approach to influential figures like the Earl of Oxford and Sir William Stonor, who she thought had abused their authority, and she readily interceded with her husband to win favours for institutions and individuals who sought her assistance. She would not have known when – if ever – Edward would recover his kingdom, but may have heard after a time that the Duke of Burgundy (their brother-in-law) had promised ships and money, and that other members of the family were pressurising the Duke of Clarence to desert Warwick. Edward returned to England on 14 March 1471 and by a combination of duplicity and decisiveness – aided by mistrust and uncertainty among his enemies – brought Warwick to battle at Barnet on 30 April. The Earl and his brother were both slain and King Henry again made prisoner; but the dust had hardly settled when Edward heard that Queen Margaret had landed at Weymouth and was raising troops. A rapid march confined the Lancastrians to the western bank of the Severn, and Margaret's forces were decisively defeated at Tewkesbury on 4 May. The Lancastrian Prince Edward was killed, either in the battle or in the rout that followed it, and Henry VI died mysteriously – or perhaps not so mysteriously – the same night that the victorious Yorkists returned to London. His life had been safe while his son lived to inherit his royal title, but with the prince dead it could be brought to an end.

Edward IV should perhaps be regarded as no more than an anti- or alternative ruler for the duration of his first reign, since Henry VI never formally abdicated, but he was indisputably king from 1471 onwards. One of his first acts after his fortunate recovery of his throne was to create his newborn son Prince of Wales and provide him with a council headed for all practical purposes by Queen Elizabeth, her brother Earl Rivers, and the ecclesiastic John Alcock. Elizabeth's new role was clearly more than a sinecure, since she accompanied her little son when a separate household was established for him at Ludlow in February 1473, went with him to Hereford to help investigate a spate of murders and robberies both there and in Shropshire, and may have been at Shrewsbury for the same reason when she gave birth to Prince Richard in August. Richard is said to have been born in the Dominican or Black friary, 'the which frears standethe under Sainct Mary's church in the sayde towne estward'[1] according to a local chronicle, but whether this was really the King and Queen's intention is uncertain. The ordinances 'as to what Preparation is to be made against the Deliveraunce of a Queen', which Lady Margaret Beaufort drew up some years afterwards, dealt with the decoration of the royal chambers and matters such as the exclusion of men from them in great detail, while other rules governed the manner in which the prince (or princess) was to be christened. The church was to be hung with arras and cloth of gold and carpeted, the child was to be baptised by a bishop or archbishop in a silver font, he was to be carried by a duchess while an earl bore the 'trayne of his mantell', and 200 torches were to be lighted as soon as the ceremony was concluded.[2] It would be surprising if all or much of this could be accomplished in a priory, however substantial, and it is possible to speculate that the boy was born prematurely before Elizabeth had any opportunity to return to London or at least the headquarters of the Principality at Ludlow. Kings, Edward IV included, had favoured the Black friars and accepted their hospitality on previous occasions, but Richard 'of Shrewsbury' was the first – and the last – royal baby to be delivered under their roof.

Richard was only the 'spare' in the line of succession, but his upbringing would have been carefully managed and his future planned from almost the moment of his birth. His father created him Duke of York on 28 May 1474 (when he was only nine months old) in a grand ceremony concluded by a tournament. This allowed Earl Rivers, the child's uncle, to demonstrate his martial abilities, but not before some of the participants had complained that the entry fees were excessive! A revised scale of charges was agreed 'for that time' – Edward could not allow such a splendid occasion to be marred by wrangling over money – and the Chancellor helped to ensure a good attendance by adjourning Parliament. His official reason was that the members might 'more quietly and devoutly' observe the feast of Pentecost, but Miss Scofield is probably correct in her assumption that 'the legislators of the land probably went to the tournament field before they went to church'![3]

We can glimpse something of King Edward's plans for Richard in the will he drew up before mounting his invasion of France in 1475. The boy was to receive three great estates, either when he came of age in 1489 (when he would have been 16), or when the existing charges upon them were quitted. He would inherit Duchy of Lancaster lands in Norfolk when his mother died, estates belonging to the Duchy of York in Northamptonshire, Lincolnshire and Rutland, principally Fotheringhay, Grantham and Stamford, on the death of his grandmother Cecily, and Lancastrian properties in Northamptonshire and Lincolnshire (the Honour of Bolingbroke) after they had contributed to the building of St George's Chapel, Windsor (Edward's chosen burial place), for twenty years.[4] The intention was clearly that he would become a power in the East Midlands and East Anglia, although not in the immediately foreseeable future. He would have been 18 when Queen Elizabeth died in 1492 and 21 when his grandmother finally expired three years later. But none of this was to come to pass.

Richard was not 2 years old when his role in a future Yorkist England was thus determined, but the process of preparing him for it began almost immediately. Master John Giles was granted £20 a year 'for his life' on 1 May 1476 for his good service in teaching both the King's sons Latin grammar,[5] and Richard soon had his own apartments (heated by twenty 'shides' of tall wood, eight faggots, four bundles of coal),[6] and his own council, officials and seal. He was allowed to use the Yorkist badge of a falcon within a fetterlock, but Edward IV is said to have given instructions that, in Richard's case, the lock should be portrayed slightly open to indicate that he (Edward), unlike his predecessors, has secured the Crown. It is shown thus in Wrythe's Garter Armorial (compiled *c.* 1488) and in the *c.* 1482 depiction of the Prince in the royal window in Canterbury Cathedral; but whether for this reason – or for another, altogether more subtle, one – is unclear.[7]

Richard lived with his mother, Queen Elizabeth, who had the principal say in his guiding and upbringing and who ensured

Badge and arms of Prince Richard of York with open fetterlock (from British Library Buccleuch MS Wrythe Garter Book, fo. 80, redrawn by Geoffrey Wheeler).

that he followed the same daily regimen that her husband had prescribed for Prince Edward. The Prince of Wales's household at Ludlow was supervised by his maternal uncle Earl Rivers, and the parts of the ordinances that applied to Edward but not to Richard have been placed in angled brackets in the following quotation:

First. We will that our <said first-begotten> son shall arise every morning at a convenient hour, according to his age; and, till he be ready, no man be suffered to come into his chamber, except <the right trusty the Earl Rivers> his chaplains, and chamberlains, or such others as shall be thought <by the said Earl Rivers> convenient for the same season; which chaplains shall say matins in his presence; and, when he is ready, and the matins said, forthwith to go to his chapel or closet, to have his mass there, and in no wise in his chamber without a cause reasonable; and no man to interrupt him during his mass-time. . . .

Item. We will that our <said> son have his breakfast immediately after his mass; and between that and his meat, to be occupied in such virtuous learning as his age shall suffer to receive. And that he be at his dinner at a convenient hour, and thereat to be honourably served, and his dishes to be borne by worshipful folks and squires, having on our livery; and that all other officers and servants give their due attendance, according to their offices.

Item. That no man sit at his board, but such as shall be thought fit <by the discretion of the Earl Rivers>; and that then be read before him such noble stories as behoveth a prince to understand and know; and that the communication at all times in his presence be of virtue, honour, cunning [knowledge], wisdom, and deeds of worship, and of nothing that should move or stir him to vice.

Item. We will that after his meat, in eschewing of idleness, he be occupied about his learning; and after, in his presence, be showed all such convenient disports and exercises, as behoveth his estate to have experience in.

Item. We will that our son go to his even-song at a convenient hour; and that soon after done, to be at his supper, and thereat to be served according as before.

Item. We will that after his supper he have all such honest disports as may be conveniently devised for his recreation.

Item. We will that our <said> son be in his chamber, and for all night livery to be set,[8] the travers [curtains] drawn anon upon eight of the clock, and all persons from thence then to be avoided, except such as shall be deputed and appointed to give their attendance upon him all night; and that they enforce themselves to make him merry and joyous towards his bed.[9]

Other rules required him to hear sermons preached on feast days, and obliged his servants and others living in his household to behave in a suitably decorous manner. No sanctions were mentioned – it was unthinkable that the King's orders would be disobeyed.

Such a carefully regulated environment appears dull, almost stifling, by modern-day standards, but it seems to have had the desired effect. Rui de Sousa, the Portuguese ambassador, remembered Richard as an ideal prince when he gave evidence at Setubal many years later, and the contemporary portrait in the Royal Window in Canterbury Cathedral shows a serious child, crowned and wearing an ermine-trimmed cloak, kneeling at prayer (see plate 1). De Sousa was asked if he had known Prince Richard when he was in England, 'to which he answered that he had seen him singing with his mother and one of his sisters and that he sang very well and that he was very pretty and the most beautiful creature he had ever seen, and he also saw him playing very well at sticks and with a two-handed sword'.[10] The Canterbury image portrays him straight-backed, with a mass-book before him, displaying the humility with which he approached both God and his earthly father, King Edward. It is a formal, stylised picture, but there is no reason to doubt that he appeared thus on state and ceremonial occasions looking older than his 8 or 9 years.[11]

Royal children featured in marriage negotiations from almost the moment they were born (from even before they were born in some cases), but it frequently happened that betrothals were cancelled long before the arrangements came to fruition. Agreements were broken in favour of new alliances as the balance of power in Europe shifted, and none of Richard's three surviving elder siblings had been married, or seemed likely to be married in the near future, when their father died in 1483. Contemporaries would have supposed that when the Prince of Wales had been successfully joined to one of the great heiresses of Europe a foreign bride of perhaps lesser standing would be found for his younger brother; but a new opportunity beckoned when the last Mowbray Duke of Norfolk died in January 1476 leaving his vast inheritance to his 3-year-old daughter Anne. King Edward lost no time in proposing that Anne should wed Prince Richard, but the widowed Duchess proved a shrewd bargainer. Richard received the earldom of Nottingham (one of the late Duke's subsidiary titles) on 12 June 1476, but if the discussions had by then made progress they were probably not finalised much before the following 7 February, when he was created Duke of Norfolk, Earl Marshal and Earl Warenne. Even then a dispensation had to be obtained from Rome before the marriage could be solemnised (Anne's great-grandmother and Richard's grandmother were sisters), and many more months passed before all the formalities were completed. Parliament was to meet at Westminster in the middle of January 1478, and it was decided that it would be appropriate for the 4-year-old groom and his 5-year-old bride to be married when many of the great and the good would be on hand to attend the ceremony. We do not know if the young couple liked, or even knew, one another at this stage, and it is doubtful if anyone tried to explain the nature of the commitment or ask them if they consented to it. It was inconceivable that either of them would refuse.

A description of this grand occasion, written, possibly, by a herald and preserved in the Ashmolean Museum, tells how on

the fourteenth day of January, the high and excellent Princesse [Anne] came to the place of estate, in the King's great chamber at Westminster, and there, according to her high and excellent estate, had a void [repast] after the forme and estate of this famous realm of England; accompanyed with many great estates and degrees, dukes and earles, and barons, and with great abundance of ladies and gentlewomen; and the Princesse before rehearsed was led by the right noble Count, Rivers. And on the morne, on Thursday the fifteenth day of the same moneth, this high Princesse before rehearsed came out of the Queenes chamber at Westminster, and so proceeded through the Kings great chamber, and into the White Hall, and so proceeded into Saint Stephens Chappell, being attended by great estates and many ladyes and gentlewomen, my lord the noble Count of Lincolne ledd her on the right hand, and upon the second hand the noble Count Rivers. And at her entry into the chappell before rehearsed, which was richly garnished with tappetts [carpets] of azure culler, inramplished [covered] with flower de luces of gould curiously wrought; and also a little space within the dore of the same chappell, there was an imperiall of cloth of gould, in manner of a canopie; and under the saide canopie was the King, the Queene, and my Lord the Prince [Edward], and the right high and excellent Princesse and Queene of right, Cicelie Mother to the Kinge, the Lady Elizabeth, the Lady Mary, the Lady Cicely, daughters to the King our Soveraigne Lord; and there was my said Lady received by Doctour Goldwell, Bishop of Norwiche. And when hee had received her in at the chappell dore, intending to proceed to her wedding, Doctor Cooke spake, and said that the high and mighty Prince Richard Duke of Yorke ought not to be wedded to that high and excellent Princesse, for that they were within [prohibited] degrees of marriage; the one at the fourth, the other at the third; for which cause hee defended [forbad] the espousalls, without that there were a speciall lycence from the Pope, and dispensacion from the Pope for the said neerenes of blood. Then Doctour Gunthorpe, Deane of the Kings Chappell, shewed an ample bull of authority, that they might proceede to the contracte and matrimony before rehersed. Thereupon the said Bishoppe of Norwiche proceeded to the marriage, and asked who should give the Princesse to the church and to him; and the King gave her, and so proceeded to the high altar to masse.[12]

The document goes on to describe how Richard, Duke of Gloucester, cast gold and silver coins 'amongest the comone people' before escorting the new bride to her wedding breakfast, where everyone sat in strict order of precedence. The author remarked that 'the presse was soe great that I might not see to write the names of them that served; the abundance of the noble people was so innumerable', and there was doubtless similar interest when King Edward created twenty-four new knights of the Bath on Sunday, 18 January, and when the celebrations concluded with a great tournament the following Thursday. Curiously, Prince Richard is unnoticed (unless, of course, his elder brother was absent and he was 'my Lord the Prince' who stood or sat beneath the canopy with his parents), and he was probably carried except when he was required to place a ring on his little bride's finger. It was Anne who was bringing her great wealth into the Yorkist royal family and all the emphasis was on her.[13]

The little couple may have kept some sort of company together in the palace at Greenwich, but their married life was of short duration. Anne died on 19 November 1481, three weeks before her ninth birthday, leaving Richard a widower at the age of 8. Her lands and titles would normally have passed to her kinsmen, John, Lord Howard, and William, Viscount Berkeley, but King Edward had ensured that his younger son would continue to hold them. An Act of Parliament of 1478 had given Richard a life interest in the estates if Anne died childless, and, although the King had 'bought' Berkeley's consent by agreeing to pay his debts to the Talbots (debts amounting to the vast sum of £34,000), Howard, who had served the dynasty long and loyally, received only a single manor.[14] It is hardly surprising that he supported Richard of Gloucester's bid for the Crown in 1483.

It is possible that a friendship had developed between the little couple in the near four years they had been married and that Richard felt a sense of loss at her passing. He was almost certainly present when she was laid to rest in the chapel dedicated to St Erasmus in Westminster Abbey (Miss Scofield points out that her funeral, which cost £215 16*s* 10*d*, must have been almost as grand as her wedding[15]), but there was little time for pause or reflection. The daily round of study continued, and his multifarious responsibilities now extended to formally witnessing charters, presenting clergy to livings of which he was patron, and fulfilling his role as lieutenant of Ireland.[16] All decisions were necessarily made for him, but the gifts and rewards he received from his father in the twentieth year of his reign (4 March 1480–3 March 1481) suggest that King Edward was pleased with his progress. 'The right high and myghty Prynce the Duke of Yorke' received a yard and a quarter of 'velvet uppon velvet grene clothe of golde' for covering a saddle and harness on 28 April, together with 'v yerdes of blac satyn and v yerdes of purpulle velvet for lynyng of the same gown, [and] v yerdes of grene satyn for a gowne, and ij yerdes di' of blac sarsinett [fine, soft silk], for lynyng of the same gowne' on 2 June. These were followed by a 'mantelle of blue velvet lined with white damask garnissht with a garter of ruddeur' (an unidentified material[17]), together with a lase (sash) of blue silk with 'botons of golde', and enough material to make him gowns of purple velvet, green velvet, green damask and white cloth when he was admitted to the Order of the Garter on 17 August, his seventh birthday. Prince Edward, his elder brother, received only 5 yards of white cloth of gold during the same period, although there is no reason to doubt that he also observed his parents' wishes and satisfied their expectations.[18] Perhaps Richard was the apple of their eye?

This well-dressed young prince was 9 in 1482, old enough to begin to appreciate and savour both his privileged position and his future role as his brother's chief, most-trusted lieutenant. It was always possible that the Prince of Wales would have an accident or succumb to illness, but if Richard ever wondered if *he* might become king one day he kept his thoughts well hidden. He behaved respectfully towards the many great men he encountered at court and on his travels, but the person he most admired was (in all probability) his maternal uncle Anthony, Earl Rivers. Rivers, soldier, scholar, administrator, governor of the Prince of Wales, and knight errant *par excellence*, was one of the most cultured men of his era. Richard had seen him fight in tournaments and may have handled copies of the books he translated; but this golden figure was seldom in London except on great occasions, and it was perhaps the boy's younger uncle, Sir Edward Woodville, another noted jouster, or more probably his elder half-brothers, Thomas, Marquess of Dorset, and Lord Richard Grey, who became his principal role models. Dorset and Lord Richard were in their twenties, resplendent, sophisticated and the companions of his father's leisure, men who caught a young boy's imagination because he knew nothing of what others said of them.[19] They humoured and indulged him, unlike his father's brother Richard, Duke of Gloucester, whose periodic, possibly dour appearances were marked by a wearisome polite formality. Uncle Richard was a successful warrior who had recaptured Berwick, but young Richard hardly knew him and may not have counted him a friend.

The next few years would be challenging and interesting and Richard probably anticipated them eagerly; but no sooner had he begun the transition from childhood to maturity than his world started to unravel. Anne's death perhaps dampened his spirits for several months afterwards, and his sadness may not have entirely faded when Mary, his second eldest sister, died suddenly on 23 May 1482. It is likely that she, Elizabeth and Cecily had petted and played with him in his infancy, and her lavish funeral was another reminder that grandeur could appear hollow and life seem cruel. Worse still, his father, King Edward, had grown corpulent and now looked much older than his forty years. In the ordinary way the King would have been expected to live for at least another decade, but he passed to his maker after a short illness on 9 April 1483. The harmonious scene described by the Croyland chronicler – 'a royal Court such as befitted a mighty kingdom, filled with riches and men from almost every nation, and (surpassing all else) with the handsome and most delightful children born of the marriage . . . to Queen Elizabeth'[20] – was really a veneer, no thicker than the paper on which it was written. Edward's death was to unleash forces he had only dimly anticipated, forces would change, and in some cases devastate, the lives of all his offspring. Richard's career as a prince of the blood was all but over by April 1483.

# FOUR

## Uncle Richard

Richard, Duke of Gloucester, afterwards King Richard III, uncle to the young Richard, Duke of York, and supposed father of Richard of Eastwell, is one of history's greatest enigmas. Generations of historians have wrestled with the problem of how a loyal royal brother could be transformed, almost overnight, into a treacherous usurper; and assessments of his motives and character have filled countless pages of books and journals. Much of the debate has been decidedly 'pro' or 'anti' – some authors have been concerned more with proving a theory than with discovering the individual whose frame of mind may have determined the way in which events unfolded – and it is worth looking again at what we know of Richard from a critical but dispassionate standpoint. This may allow us to discern a man who was perhaps not always worthy of the admiration bestowed by his modern supporters, but whose actions can be explained in terms of the milieu in which he operated; a man who arguably ordered a number of murders, but who may not have been guilty of the most notorious of all.

Richard was born at Fotheringhay Castle in Northamptonshire on 2 October 1452, the eleventh of the twelve children that Cecily Neville, called by later generations the 'Rose of Raby', bore her husband, Richard, Duke of York. It was only six months since York had faced the King at Dartford in the first confrontation of the Wars of the Roses, and the child emerged into a world of violent clashes punctuated by temporary truces in which privilege and insecurity went hand in hand. He was only 7 when, in October 1459, his father fled into the night from Ludlow, leaving his family to throw themselves on the mercy of the triumphant Lancastrians. Richard, his mother and elder brother George were placed in the custody of the Duchess of Buckingham, who 'kept them straight with many a great rebuke';[1] and it was not until the following summer that the Yorkist victory at Northampton allowed Duke Richard to return from exile and claim the Crown. The compromise that would have allowed Henry VI to remain king while disinheriting his son was rejected by Queen Margaret, and York and his son, Edmund, Earl of Rutland (Richard's elder brother), were killed at Wakefield on the last day of 1460. Duchess Cecily sent her two youngest sons to Burgundian territory for safety when Margaret's forces subsequently threatened London; and, although the Duke of Burgundy treated the now fatherless boys kindly, their futures hung in the balance until Edward, their eldest brother, crushed their enemies at Towton on Palm Sunday 1461.

There is nothing to suggest that these events damaged Richard psychologically – such evidence seldom survives from so remote a period – but they surely made a lasting impression on him. The misfortunes that had buffeted his family in the past year and a half may have affected him more than his elder siblings, and it would not be surprising if, henceforward, he felt a profound sense of insecurity when he believed he was threatened. His brother recalled him to England, made him a knight of the Bath and, at the age of 9, created him Duke of

Gloucester; but honours could be cancelled as easily as they were awarded, and Richard may have already decided that when he grew to manhood he would never, so far as he was able, place himself in the hands of others or take loyalty for granted. When the need arose, he would strike first and strike decisively, leaving as little as possible to the wiles of fortune. He could always make amends or excuses if events showed that he had feared too much.

Richard had now reached an age when he could begin his formal knightly training, and in November 1461 he set out on the long journey to the Earl of Warwick's castle of Middleham in north Yorkshire.[2] Aristocratic children were routinely sent away from home into other households to learn self-reliance and bond with those whose comradeship would prove valuable later, but King Edward's decision to entrust his youngest brother's development to his greatest subject would affect more than Richard's education. It was at Middleham that the boy first encountered Anne Neville, the Earl's younger daughter, whom he would later marry; that he began his lifelong association with the north and things northern; and where he was captivated by Warwick's personal magnificence. When the King entertained some visiting Bohemian knights to a sixty-course dinner, the Earl subsequently placed seventy courses before them; and the banquet held at Cawood Castle after George Neville, Warwick's brother, had been enthroned as Archbishop of York has been dubbed the greatest feast of the Middle Ages. A youngster could not fail to admire, and be influenced by, such opulence, but the new, secure world they represented was not to last.

We have already noticed King Edward's marriage to Elizabeth Woodville and the consequences of the Kingmaker's dissatisfaction, but not the effect these events had upon Richard personally. Paul Murray Kendall speculates that he shared Warwick's dislike of the Queen and her numerous family, but, when faced with a stark choice between his admired tutor and his beloved elder brother, committed himself entirely to Edward. This may be true to some extent – Richard shared the royal exile in Holland and fought against Warwick at Barnet – but there is no firm evidence that he was on bad terms with the Woodvilles in his brother's lifetime. Kendall's view of Elizabeth as 'rapacious' and 'haughty' has been largely discounted by more recent historians,[3] and Richard was cooperating amicably with her brother Anthony, Earl Rivers, as late as March 1483.[4] Perhaps he would not countenance treason, even when it was committed by a former friend and mentor, but his decision may have been influenced by the realisation that he would have little security in an England dominated by Queen Margaret. He has been commended for his loyalty to Edward and rightly so, but only Edward's success would secure his position and further his prospects. Supporting Warwick was no option at all.

The battles of Barnet and Tewkesbury gave the 18-year-old Richard a baptism of fire as a military commander, and the aftermath of Tewkesbury provided him with his first lessons in political ruthlessness. A number of senior Lancastrians sought refuge from King Edward's victorious forces in the abbey church in the belief that their lives would be safe there; but the sanctuary lacked the privilege of either a papal bull or a royal charter, and they were persuaded, or compelled, to submit to justice. They were tried before Richard, acting in his capacity as Constable of England, condemned, and sentenced to suffer immediate execution; and we can only wonder how the young judge felt as the heads of these men, some of them former acquaintances and colleagues, rolled in the dust before him. He must surely have reflected that he would now be experiencing the last moments of his own earthly existence if fortune had dictated otherwise, and that henceforward he could expect no mercy if events turned against him. His youth, and the allowances traditionally made for youth, ended with

Tewkesbury. Kind-heartedness was a luxury he could no longer afford.

Richard's condemnation of his defeated opponents in the aftermath of the battle had been formal and legal, but he has been accused of being less scrupulous in his dealings with Edward, the Lancastrian Prince of Wales, and with the youth's father, Henry VI. The popular legend is that the Prince was captured, brought before Edward IV, and done to death by Richard and other noblemen; but the chroniclers, both Yorkist and Lancastrian, are quite adamant that he was slain 'in the pursuit' and 'in the field'.[5] His father's death is more problematical, since Henry seems to have expired the very night the victorious Yorkist army returned to London when Richard 'and many other' were at the Tower.[6] The Yorkist apologist wrote that the old King had died of 'pure displeasure and melencoly'[7] when he was told of what had happened at Tewkesbury, but his death was surely too convenient to have been anything other that a private execution. It is impossible to say what part, if any, Richard may have played in this unfortunate business, but he could have been no more than a messenger and observer. It was King Edward who had decided that Henry should be eliminated, and who had taught his younger brother that expediency could take precedence over legality when personal and dynastic issues were at stake.

The destruction of the Lancastrian and Neville opposition set the House of York still more firmly on the throne of England, but the first years of Edward IV's second reign were marred by the fierce rivalry that developed between Richard and their brother George, Duke of Clarence, for the lion's share of the Warwick inheritance. Richard was granted the Kingmaker's northern Neville estates (lands that would have passed to the latter's brother or nephew if he had not committed treason), while George, who had married Warwick's elder daughter Isabel, was given the Beauchamp-Despenser estates of his

Countess, Anne Beauchamp. The Countess, who was in sanctuary at Beaulieu Abbey, protested that her lands were being redistributed although she had not offended the Crown personally, and was hardly reassured when Richard let it be known that he intended to marry Anne, her younger daughter, and claim half the inheritance from Clarence! Clarence, too, was furious and was heard to declare that 'he [Richard] may weell have my Ladye hys suster in lawe, butt they schall parte no lyvelod [property]',[8] but his younger brother was perhaps more determined than he realised. Richard discovered Anne concealed in the house of one of Clarence's followers 'disguised in the habit of a cookmaid', according to the Croyland writer,[9] and took her to the sanctuary of St Martin le Grand while he pleaded his case with King Edward. The outcome was that he married Anne and was promised some of the estates that still legally belonged to her mother; but he had to surrender the Great Chamberlainship of England to Clarence, who was also granted the earldoms of Salisbury and Warwick.[10]

This should, of course, have been the end of the matter, but George of Clarence proved reluctant to implement what he regarded as a less favourable settlement. The King leaned on him by releasing the Countess of Warwick into Richard's custody and by not exempting him from a resumption of royal grants, but this seems to have only exacerbated his sense of injustice. Sir John Paston reported in November 1473 that 'ffor the most part that be abowt the Kyng have sende hyddr ffor ther harneys, and it [is] seyd ffor serteyn, that the Duke off Clarence makyth hym bygge in that he kan, schewyng as he wolde but dele with the Duke of Glowcester; but the Kyng ententyth, in eschyewying all inconvenyents, to be as bygge as they bothe, and to be a styffeler atweyn them . . . so what shall falle, can I nott seye'.[11] We do not know how Edward persuaded his brothers to desist from armed conflict, but in May 1474 an Act of Parliament gave force of law to the 1472 settlement by depriving the Countess of Warwick of her estates and conferring them on her two sons-in-law as though she were already dead. It restored many of Clarence's resumed lands while protecting both brothers against future legislation, and the King doubtless hoped that there would be no more problems. But Clarence had lost some property (part of the Beauchamp-Despenser inheritance and the Duchy of Lancaster Honour of Tutbury, which Edward had declined to restore to him), while Richard had not gained everything he wished to have.

It is unclear why it took so long to settle this vexed matter, but it may have been at least partly because Richard and Anne were related to each other within the prohibited degrees. They were blood relatives (first cousins, once removed), related in the second and third degrees of consanguinity; but the dispensation issued to them on 22 April 1472 covered only a more distant relationship by marriage. They would surely have tried to persuade the Pope to issue the more comprehensive document they needed after their wedding, and the 1474 Act of Parliament noted 'that yf the seid Richard Duke of Gloucester and Anne, bee hereafter devorced, and after the same be lawfully maried, that yet this present Acte be to theym as good and vaillable (available) as yf no such devorce had been had but as yf the same Anne had contynued wyfe to the seid Duke of Gloucester'.[12] Marie Barnfield suggests that Clarence knew that his brother and sister-in-law needed to obtain another, fuller dispensation to legalise their marriage, and may have thought that, if this proved impossible (if he could prevent it and Richard was therefore not, and had never been, Anne's lawful husband), he would not have to surrender any lands to him.[13] No evidence for this second dispensation has yet been discovered, but the wedding mentioned in *Hearne's Fragment*, ('Anne was wedded to Richard Duke of Gloucester after, in the year of our Lord 1474' (emphasis added)[14] may have been a formal remarriage after all difficulties had been finally overcome.

Richard may have felt that his uncompromising loyalty in 1470–1 justified his profiting at the expense of the then disloyal Clarence, but Clarence had helped his brother win the battles of Barnet and Tewkesbury and may have thought even his partial deprivation a poor reward. He had once been heir to both his brother and Henry VI and was now neither; but a new opportunity seemed to beckon when Charles, Duke of Burgundy, was killed at Nancy on 5 January 1477. Mary, Charles's unmarried daughter, needed a husband who would be able to use the resources of his own country to help defend her territories against Louis XI, and Duchess Margaret (the Duke's widow and King Edward's sister) suggested their brother Clarence, whose wife, Isabel, had died a few days before Christmas. Clarence was only too ready to exchange his dull and rather pointless existence for a role in the theatre of European politics, but Edward dismissed the matter out of hand. He had no intention of compromising either the annual pension that Louis had agreed to pay him after he had withdrawn his forces from France in 1475 or the agreement that his eldest daughter would marry the Dauphin, and may have believed the French King when he hinted that Clarence would one day use Burgundian arms to seize power in England. The Duke was bitterly disappointed and retired to his estates, where he behaved in a generally lawless and threatening manner until, finally, he was arrested and sent to the Tower in June 1477.[15] He was tried in Parliament the following January and convicted of a number of offences, including spreading rumours that Edward was not entitled to the throne because he was allegedly a bastard,[16] and the more serious charge of secretly preserving an exemplification of the agreement that recognised him as heir to the throne if Henry VI's line failed. Professor Lander has argued persuasively that this last charge was effectively invented by Edward, implying that the King had another, more valid, reason for destroying his brother that could not be mentioned in public. It is possible that Bishop Stillington had revealed to Clarence – what he was later to reveal to Richard of Gloucester – that Edward and Elizabeth Woodville were not legally married and their children could not, therefore, inherit the throne. This allegation, if true, would have allowed Clarence to claim the kingdom on Edward's death, and may be the real reason why he was executed on 18 February 1478.

Richard can have seen little of Clarence during the last few years of the latter's lifetime, and we do not know if he thought Edward's action precipitate or accepted that he had little choice. Kendall has him pleading with the King to pardon their brother, but there is no evidence that he actually did so. He might, conceivably, have been glad to see the back of a dangerous rival, and was content to accept the great chamberlainship (which he had surrendered to Clarence six years earlier) and the earldom of Salisbury for his own son, Edward. Dominic Mancini wrote in 1483 that the Duke of Gloucester came only rarely to court after Clarence's execution, implying that he blamed the Queen and her kin for what had happened; but Richard was much occupied with the wars in Scotland in the years after 1478, and Mancini may have assumed that his harsh treatment of the Woodvilles after he seized power owed something to his brother's execution. Richard undoubtedly blamed the Queen's family for encouraging Edward's licentiousness and accused them of plotting his own downfall, but he never charged them with engineering Clarence's death.[17]

When King Edward died, unexpectedly, on 9 April 1483, Richard of Gloucester was at Middleham, Prince Edward (now Edward V) and his uncle Rivers were at Ludlow, and Queen Elizabeth, her son Prince Richard, and a number of senior noblemen (including the Marquess of Dorset and William, Lord

Hastings) were in London. Edward's last will has vanished, but it is likely that in it he had named his brother protector during his son's minority, although without diminishing Earl Anthony's authority with regard to his person or excluding the Queen from the role she had been given in his original testament drawn up in 1475. He was aware that, in all probability, there would be some jostling for power between the Woodvilles and those noblemen who had always considered them upstarts, but hoped they would put aside their differences in the interests of his 12-year-old son. The Queen and her relatives were prepared to share power with Richard – Mancini tells us that they proposed that 'the government should be carried on by many persons among whom the duke, far from being excluded, should be accounted the chief'[18] – but either he did not trust them or could not accept a situation in which the boy-king's mind could be managed or swayed by others. The result was the dramatic scene at Northampton where Richard and Rivers had arranged to meet en route to London. They shared an amicable supper in the company of Richard's kinsman the Duke of Buckingham, but next morning Rivers found his lodgings surrounded by armed soldiers. The dukes then dashed 14 miles to Stony Stratford, where they arrested other Woodvilles and assured Edward, who was there with them, that they were acting in his best interests. The boy is said to have expressed considerable scepticism, but had no alternative but to do as his uncles wished.[19]

It seems clear that it was Richard who was conspiring against the Woodvilles rather than vice versa (we have only his word for it that the four wagonloads of weapons he brought to London were to have been used against him), and it is possible to argue that it was his deeply ingrained sense of insecurity that compelled him to act against them at Northampton and Stony Stratford. Richard's protectorship would have lasted only until Edward V was crowned on 4 May (the date already determined by the councillors assembled in London), after which the Council – in effect, a council of regency – would have governed on behalf of the young sovereign until he could begin to rule personally in three or four years' time. He would, of course, exercise a growing influence over decisions taken during this interval, and would inevitably prefer and lend support to councillors drawn from his mother's family, the people who had brought him up and were already his intimates. Richard probably feared that this would lead to his own exclusion from the government, and he had the example of his predecessor as Duke of Gloucester, Duke Humphrey, always before him. Humphrey had been denied the regency of England that his brother, Henry V, had desired for him, and had eventually been done to death at Bury St Edmunds in 1447, probably with the connivance of Henry VI, his nephew, and Henry's Beaufort half-blood relatives. Duke Richard may have feared that his relationship with Edward V and *his* half-brothers would be similarly troubled, and there was a real likelihood that he would meet the same end.

This was one concern for Richard: another was that his title to many of his landholdings was not as secure or as permanent as he would have liked. His grant of Warwick the Kingmaker's personal estates would revert to a life interest if the heir male, George Neville, died childless (to protect the residual rights of other members of the Neville family), and his share of his mother-in-law's Beauchamp-Despenser inheritance was held on behalf of his wife, Anne and, after her, their son, Edward. There was no danger while they lived or as long as he retained political authority; but he would have been acutely conscious of his wife and son's frailty and may have known that George Neville was seriously ill when he seized Edward V at Stony Stratford. He may have decided that extending his protectorship into the foreseeable future was the only way of preventing other Nevilles from claiming that they had a better right to the lands if the worst happened; and his fears were justified when George died in May 1483, Edward in April 1484 and Anne in March 1485. By then, of course, he was king and his position unassailable; but it could have been a very different story if his influence had been in decline.

The same was also true of some of Richard's other landholdings, which he had acquired by doubtful or even coercive methods. He had been granted the estates of the Lancastrian Earl of Oxford and his brothers after Barnet, but had no intention of leaving a third of them (the recognised portion) in the hands of Oxford's mother, the dowager countess. The old lady was taken into custody and compelled to surrender both these and her own estates to him under threat of being sent to Middleham in the depths of winter; and even King Edward warned a prospective purchaser not to risk buying one of the properties 'though the title of the place be good in my brother of Gloucester's hands'. Richard was assured of the lands only as long as he remained powerful or Oxford continued to oppose the Yorkist dynasty; and it was possible that the Earl would one day make his peace with King Edward and seek restoration as a loyal subject. William Tunstall, one of Richard's northern retainers, told the dowager 'that the said duke was a knight and a king's brother and he trusted that he would do her no wrong', but either he was simply trying to comfort her or, like others, assumed that his master would play by the rules.[20] Similarly, George Neville was degraded from the peerage in 1478 when he was about to attain his majority, a decision that effectively prevented him from challenging Richard for *his* inheritance. Richard secured his wardship and marriage two years later, and Paul Murray Kendall thought that looking after the interests of a young man who had neither parents nor property was an act of kindness. It may have been, but there can be little doubt that Richard recognised the advantages of keeping a potential rival in his own hands.[21]

Some writers have argued that Richard intended to make a bid for the throne from the very beginning, but there is nothing to suggest that he meant to depose his nephew at this stage of the proceedings. The two dukes bestowed every courtesy on young Edward as they escorted him to London, and, although his coronation was postponed (inevitably, since the royal party reached the capital only on 4 May), summonses were issued and clothes ordered as though everything was now settled. Another man might have acted more calmly and pragmatically, but Richard's fears had led him to behave in a manner that was as unexpected as it was unprecedented. Earl Rivers, an astute and experienced politician, had walked blindly into the trap prepared for him, and news of the arrests at Northampton and Stony Stratford so surprised and alarmed Queen Elizabeth that she rushed into sanctuary with her family. Now, more than ever, Richard was determined to deal with any perceived threat to what he regarded as his rightful position and security before his supposed enemies or rivals could deal with him.

The Woodvilles had either failed to realise that Richard mistrusted them or thought him incapable of such decisive, ruthless action; and it is worth asking if they ought to have been more alive to the reality of the situation. Richard had been brought up in a hard school where he had learned to give, as well as to take, the blows that life dealt him, and had shown on a number of occasions that there was a determined, even cynical, streak in his character. Previously, of course, his actions had not gone beyond what may be described as 'lordly high-handedness', a common enough trait at this period; but had not Warwick the Kingmaker taken a king into custody and executed some of his relatives just as Richard was to order the deaths of Earl Rivers and the others arrested at Stony Stratford? Perhaps Rivers ought to have realised that this pupil of Warwick was as capable of doing to him what the Kingmaker had done to his father; but he may have supposed that all that was past, and that an old colleague with whom he had shared Edward IV's exile would never treat him in such a manner. If so, he was quickly disillusioned, just as others were to be disillusioned before this unfortunate business was brought to an end.

# FIVE

## *Into the Tower*

King Edward was initially lodged in the Bishop of London's palace when the royal party reached London, but was moved to the royal apartments in the Tower at some time within the next two weeks. Richard of Gloucester may have preferred to keep him well away from those he mistrusted, but there is no evidence that he meant him any harm. The Tower had not yet acquired its later, more sinister, reputation, and the assembled councillors would have thought it a secure and proper place of residence for their young sovereign. They agreed that Gloucester should be appointed protector 'with power to order and forbid in every matter, just like another king . . .',[1] as the Croyland chronicler has it, and the various parties settled down to await the coronation, which had been rescheduled for Sunday 22 June.

At first, matters appeared to be proceeding well enough. Gloucester demurred to the Council's decision not to charge Earl Rivers and the others arrested at Northampton and Stony Stratford with treason (because he had not been appointed protector when they had allegedly conspired against him), and appointed a committee to persuade Queen Elizabeth and her family to leave sanctuary. We know comparatively little about what happened in the weeks that followed – still less about how the Protector's mind changed as the situation altered – but his apparent confidence in the future when he first entered London had been replaced by real anxiety by the second week in June. On Monday 9 June Simon Stallworthe informed Sir William Stonor that Gloucester, Buckingham and other lords were at Westminster for four hours 'butt ther wass none that spake with the Qwene' (any longer);[2] and two days later Richard dispatched urgent messages to some northern friends asking them to come armed to London 'their to eide and assiste us ayanst the Quiene, hir blode adherentte and affinitie, which have entended, and daly doith intend, to murder and uttly distroy us, our cousyn the duc of Bukkynghm, and the old royall blode of this realme'.[3] The Woodvilles were accused of fomenting new conspiracies against him, but it was William, Lord Hastings, Edward IV's chamberlain and closest friend, who paid the supreme penalty. He was publicly and personally accused of treason at a meeting of the Council held in the Tower on the 13th, and instantly beheaded without any form of judicial process. Thomas, Lord Stanley, Archbishop Rotherham of York and Bishop Morton of Ely (who were held to be complicit with him) were arrested, and Gloucester announced that yet another conspiracy involving the Queen's family had been nipped in the bud.

The arrests at Northampton and Stony Stratford had been carefully orchestrated, and few could have doubted the reasons for them, but the murder of Hastings was as ruthless as it was inexplicable. Lord William had written to Richard shortly after Edward IV's death urging him to secure his place in the government, and had boasted that his ally had achieved this 'without causing as much blood to be shed as would be produced by a cut finger'.[4] Some writers allege that he had expected to become the Protector's principal confidant, and threw in his lot with the Woodvilles when it became apparent that Richard preferred Buckingham's counsel; but his often fraught relations with the Queen's family made them unlikely bedfellows. Thomas More tells us that Elizabeth disliked him because she thought him 'secretelye familyer with the kynge [Edward IV] in wanton coumpanye';[5] her eldest son, the Marquess of Dorset, had vied with him for the favours 'of the mistresses whom they had abducted, or attempted to entice from one another';[6] and he had engaged in a bitter, public feud with Earl Rivers after Rivers had spread rumours that he would betray Calais to the French. The only thing they had in common was their loyalty to the young King Edward, and it is difficult to avoid the conclusion that they were thrown together by the realisation that Gloucester meant to take the boy's throne from him. Hastings was perhaps the only man who had both the will and the power to frustrate Richard's purpose, and this is why he was so dramatically and bloodily removed.

But why had the Protector decided to depose his nephew when he had apparently been ready to crown him only a few weeks earlier? The ostensible reason is that Bishop Stillington had revealed to him what he had earlier told Clarence, that Edward IV's marriage to Elizabeth Woodville was invalid and their children therefore had no right to the throne. We cannot, at this distance in time, probe the validity of this allegation or explain why apparently only Stillington knew of it: but it was quite possible that Edward had entered into a 'precontract' with the Lady Eleanor Butler at some time between the death of her first husband in February 1461 and his own marriage in May 1464. A precontract was only a little less binding than marriage and invalidated a union with another person while it remained in being; but the King had never tried to amend the situation, either after Lady Butler died in 1468 or before the Prince of Wales, the future Edward V, was born in 1470.[7] It may have been only one of a number of promises he had made to various ladies, promises he had no intention of keeping and never dreamed would return to haunt his youthful successor. He had complete confidence in his younger brother, and would have supposed that he would deal with any problems that reared their heads.

What we do not know (and will probably never know) is whether Richard decided to make his bid for the throne *after* Stillington had told him that Edward V could not inherit, or whether he merely used an old rumour to justify what could not be justified in any other circumstances. Hastings and others may well have baulked at the story (or perhaps Richard feared they would do so), and refused to depose the young King on what they regarded as little more than a technicality. Bastardy, whether real or theoretical, had not prevented William the Conqueror from becoming king in 1066, nor would it prevent Queens Mary and Elizabeth from succeeding in the next century; and, if the lords wanted Edward V to reign over them, they had only to crown him or pass an appropriate Act of Parliament. Richard could have verified his assessment of the situation by referring the whole question of his brother's marriage to an ecclesiastical court, but showed no interest in doing so. He had perhaps come to realise that, while his decision to arrest Rivers and the other Woodvilles had bought him some time, his protectorship could not be extended indefinitely and Edward V could not be prevented from favouring his mother's family. The only 'solution' – the only way he could guarantee his long-term future – was to become king himself.

Hastings knew, or ought to have known, something of Richard's character, but, like Rivers, had suspected nothing. Kings had been deposed with alarming regularity since Henry Bolingbroke had seized Richard II's throne in 1399 (the number would have been still greater if the Percy and Scrope rebellions against Henry IV and the 'Southampton Plot' against Henry V had succeeded), but the royal uncles had been models of probity during Henry VI's long minority and no one thought that Richard would behave differently. Richard succeeded because his coups were staged, not against his enemies, who would have half expected them, but against men who knew him as a colleague and even as a friend. More wrote that 'the protectour loved him [Hastings] wel, and loth was to have loste him', and, although Richard had sent Earl Rivers a dish from his own table after his arrest at Northampton 'prayinge him to bee of good chere, all should be well inough',[8] Rivers was subsequently beheaded in defiance of the Council's wishes. Richard was now acting as a king (although even kings did not execute without due judicial process), and it is difficult to see his elimination of those who would have opposed his purpose as anything other than a bid for the throne.

His next step was to secure the person of Prince Richard, who was still in sanctuary with his mother and sisters. 'The spectacle of the Dowager Queen hiding her children under the wings of the Church cast an intolerable obloquy upon the government,' wrote Kendall,[9] but the Protector also realised that his opponents would not hesitate to use the younger prince as a substitute for King Edward or proclaim him king if Edward died. On 16th June, three days after Hastings's execution, Westminster was surrounded with soldiers, and a delegation of peers and churchmen led by Cardinal Bourchier, the elderly Archbishop of Canterbury, asked Elizabeth to release her son to them. The boy, they argued, ought to be present at his brother's coronation (Gloucester had not, so far, made his intentions public), and asked his mother why she thought he needed the protection of the sanctuary when he had done nothing wrong? More records the long, fruitless and perhaps partly imaginary debate that followed, a debate, he says, that was concluded only when the Archbishop told Elizabeth bluntly that, if she surrendered Prince Richard to them, he would personally guarantee the boy's safety, but that, if she refused, 'he never entended more to move her in that matter, in which she thought that he, and all other save herselfe, lacked either wit or trouth'. 'The quene with these wordes stode a good while in a great study.' She knew there was a real possibility that Gloucester would force the sanctuary if she refused to cooperate, and she did not doubt Bourchier's sincerity or his ability to protect Richard from danger. Finally, after much soul-searching, she gave her son to the assembled lords, reminding them of the trust that his father had placed in them and warning them (in More's words) that, 'as farre as ye thinke that I fere to muche, be you wel ware that you fere not as farre to little'. 'And therewith she kissed him, and blessed him, turned her back and wept and went her way, leaving the childe weping as fast.'[10]

The prince was sent to join his elder brother in the Tower, and on Sunday 22 June, one Ralph Shaa (or Shaw), a Cambridge-educated friar, preached a sermon at St Paul's Cross in which he questioned Edward V's right to the succession and argued that Richard of Gloucester was the lawful king. Mancini thought that Shaa had based his argument on Edward IV's own alleged bastardy without, perhaps, mentioning Stillington's revelation of the precontract; but the first accusation was quickly abandoned (possibly because it seriously offended Gloucester's mother) in favour of the invalidity of the late King's marriage.[11] Gloucester's claim was not, apparently, received with any real enthusiasm, but on 26 June an assembly of peers and notables, lacking a leader and mindful, no doubt, of the fate of Hastings, formally offered him the Crown. He duly accepted and was crowned King Richard III on 6 July.

Contemporary historians paid little attention to the two boys thereafter, and they simply faded into oblivion in the weeks and months that followed. Dominic Mancini wrote that, 'after Hastings was removed, all the attendants who had waited upon the king were debarred access to him. He and his brother were withdrawn into the inner apartments of the Tower proper, and day by day began to be seen more rarely behind the bars and windows, till at length they ceased to appear altogether.'[12] This appears to contradict the *Great Chronicle of London*'s comment that 'duryng this mayris yere [Edmund Shaa's, which extended from October 1482 to October 1483], the childyr of kyng Edward were seen shotyng & playyng in the gardyn of the Towyr by sundry tymys',[13] but the writer was presumably referring to the period before 13 June, when the elder boy was allowed more freedom. The well-informed Croyland continuator states that they remained in the Tower 'in the custody of certain persons appointed for that purpose'[14] until some time after Richard's son was created Prince of Wales at York on 8 September, but this is the last, informed, mention of their whereabouts and the last time they were assumed to be alive.

No one, apparently, saw or heard anything of the Princes thereafter, and it was quickly assumed that they had died. Charles Ross makes the point that fifteenth-century England was not a police state in which people could disappear only to re-emerge after many years in custody,[15] and the fates of earlier deposed kings of England made it seem unlikely that they would be allowed to survive for long. Edward II, Richard II and Henry VI had all 'disappeared' as quickly as circumstances permitted, and, although the organisers of the October uprising known as 'Buckingham's Rebellion' hoped initially to restore young Edward, they quickly accepted 'a rumour' (as the Croyland chronicler calls it)[16] that both the King and his brother were already dead. We do not know why Buckingham turned against the man he had helped to become king only a few short months earlier, but revulsion at the deaths of the Princes is only one of a number of possibilities. The Duke had his own claim to the Crown, and the suggestion that he rebelled for this reason is no more probable than the allegation that he killed the boys himself.

The rebels found an alternative candidate for the throne in the person of Henry Tudor, Henry VI's uterine half-nephew, who had lived in exile since 1471. Henry's descent from John of Gaunt's legitimated Beaufort family (a junior branch of the House of Lancaster) meant that his claim was at best tenuous, but his mother, Margaret Beaufort, worked assiduously to improve his prospects. She approached Elizabeth Woodville, using Dr Lewis Caerleon, who attended them both in his professional capacity, as her intermediary, and they agreed that Henry would marry Elizabeth's eldest daughter, Elizabeth of York, when he had ousted King Richard. Commentators have argued that Elizabeth would never have consented to this arrangement unless she believed that both her sons by King Edward had perished, but this is by no means certain. She would have found it difficult to obtain reliable information about them from within the Westminster sanctuary, and would have hoped against hope that the rumours of their deaths were unfounded. We do not know exactly what Lady Margaret proposed to Elizabeth, but she would have tried to avoid giving the impression that the present uncertainty suited her purpose or that she was seeking to promote her own son's interests at the expense of the Princes. She may have hinted that the restoration of Edward V or, failing him, his younger brother was still the conspirators' preferred option, and that Henry would claim the throne only if they were no longer able to do so. Henry would probably not have settled for anything less than the kingdom, but Margaret may have convinced Elizabeth that he would be content to become the King's brother-in-law and a great noble. Elizabeth was in no position to question her mentor's integrity, and approved the marriage on the understanding that her own sons' rights would be respected if they were found to be still alive.

The rebels drew substantial support from the south-east, the south-west and central southern England, but were defeated by a combination of poor cordination, determined opposition and bad weather. Buckingham, who had been prevented from crossing the Severn, was executed in Salisbury marketplace on 2 November, and Henry's small flotilla returned to Brittany when it became apparent that his enemies controlled the coast. Lady Margaret escaped serious punishment (Lord Stanley, her husband, was given her lands and told to ensure that she and her son had no further contact), and Queen Elizabeth and her daughters were not forcibly removed from sanctuary. Richard's anger may have cooled as the months passed (or perhaps he chose not to cause a public spectacle or further distress his nieces), and he finally reached an accord, or compromise, with his sister-in-law in March 1484. Richard promised to protect the girls, to put them 'in honest places of good name & fame' and to marry them to 'gentilmen borne' with appropriate dowries. Their mother was to have 700 marks (£466 13s 4d) a year for her lifetime, and was assured that no future allegations would be held against her until she had been given an opportunity to clear her name.[17]

Historians have argued that Elizabeth would have resented making this, or any other, agreement with the man who had so harmed her family, but realised that she had little alternative. The Church authorities may have been pressing her to leave her increasingly claustrophobic refuge, and she finally accepted that she would have to deal with Richard – who was fifteen years her junior and who would probably remain king for the rest of her lifetime – whether she liked it or not. The Croyland chronicler wrote that Elizabeth came to terms only 'after frequent entreaties as well as threats had been made use of', and Charles Ross commented that the accord, confirmed 'by the most solemn and public promise that Richard could contrive . . . reeks of the queen-dowager's suspicions',[18] but there are indications that their relationship improved after she had left sanctuary.[19] Elizabeth may indeed have felt that she had been pressurised and wondered how far she could trust Richard; but, remarkably, she then wrote to the Marquess of Dorset, the elder son of her first marriage, urging him to abandon Henry Tudor and return to England.[20] Dorset, who had joined Henry after the failure of Buckingham's rebellion, tried to slip away from his little court, but was pursued and 'persuaded' to return to Paris, where the exiles were then living. He did not, apparently, think that Richard was trying to entrap him (or that his mother was being 'used' for this purpose), and it is possible to surmise she had been able to tell him something that convinced him that the situation in London had significantly changed.

So why had Elizabeth Woodville concluded that Richard III was no longer her enemy? She may have felt that her agreement with him was satisfactory and that she had done her best for her five daughters, but this alone would not have obliterated the memory of the executions of her brother and the younger son of her first marriage or of ten months of fear and misery. The failure of Buckingham's rebellion had shattered any hope that Henry Tudor would ride to her rescue, and his mother's duplicity would have become apparent when she heard that he had been proclaimed king by his followers at Rennes Cathedral on Christmas Day 1483. This news may have reached Elizabeth in January or February and made her more inclined to come to terms with Richard, but the one thing that would have really changed her attitude towards him was the prospect of being reunited with at least one of her sons. King Richard may have revealed to her that Edward, the elder boy, had died from natural causes, but that Richard, the younger, was in safe custody and would be allowed to join her when she left sanctuary. The arrangement had to remain secret, of course (which is why it was not mentioned in their formal agreement), and it is not inconceivable that Richard also hinted that the boy might succeed him if his own son died and he had no other children. The Prince of Wales did in fact die about 9 April, and Elizabeth could well have convinced herself that everything would come right in the end.

We do not, unfortunately, know where Elizabeth (and presumably her younger daughters)[21] went after they left Westminster, but there are two possibilities. The King had entrusted the guarding of the sanctuary to John Nesfield, one of his squires of the body, and the agreement implies that he was to remain at least nominally responsible for her. Nesfield was a Yorkshireman, but Richard had given him the manor of Haytesbury in Wiltshire at the beginning of his reign, and it was perhaps to Haytesbury that Elizabeth was now taken.[22] A house well away from London where John could keep an eye on her and report anything untoward would have suited Richard's purpose admirably, and the same would apply when her younger son joined her, perhaps in the late spring of 1484. But by June or July Nesfield was in Scarborough preparing to lead the King's navy against the French and Scots, and his brief capture may have caused Richard to place Elizabeth and her son in the custody of another trusted retainer, Sir James Tyrell. We have already noticed the tradition that the former Queen and some of her children lived at Gipping Hall, Sir James's house near Stowmarket, in Suffolk, 'by permission of the uncle', and this is by no means improbable.[23] Stowmarket is about the same distance from the capital as Haytesbury, and Tudor stories that Tyrell had murdered the boys nine months before he became Prince Richard's protector can be dismissed as so much speculation. Elizabeth probably hoped that this move would prove to be more permanent, but Tyrell, like Nesfield, had many other responsibilities. His appointment as commander of Guisnes Castle, one of the fortresses defending Calais, in January 1485, would have made it virtually impossible for him to supervise his charges personally, and they may have been moved to a third, unknown location shortly afterwards. We will probably never know for certain, but Elizabeth and her children had to live somewhere and there is at least some evidence to connect her with Nesfield and Tyrell and with their homes.

Elizabeth had known little peace since the death of King Edward, and her wheel of fortune threatened to spin still more violently as 1484 turned to 1485. Richard's wife, Queen Anne, was unlikely to bear him any more children, and eyebrows were raised when he invited Princess Elizabeth of York to join the court to celebrate the Christmas season. The younger Elizabeth stands out because the Croyland continuator spoke, disapprovingly, of how she and Queen Anne exchanged dresses. 'Too much attention [he says] was paid to singing and dancing and to vain exchanges of clothing between Queen Anne and Lady Elizabeth, eldest daughter of the dead king, who were alike in complexion and figure'.[24] The two ladies were evidently on good terms with each other, and many of those present (Anne included) would have regarded the switches as a piece of light-hearted amusement. But were there also those who recognised the implied meaning that, if Elizabeth could step into Anne's clothes so easily, she could step as effortlessly into her role as queen?

These suggestions could be dismissed as mere speculation, but there is evidence that Richard did at least consider marrying the princess in order to frustrate Henry Tudor. The Croyland writer comments that 'it was said by many that the king was applying his mind in every way to contracting a marriage with Elizabeth [of York] either after the death of the queen, or by means of a divorce for which he believed he had sufficient grounds'.[25] Richard's seventeenth-century biographer Sir George Buck was shown a letter written by Elizabeth to John Howard, whom the King had created Duke of Norfolk, in

February 1485. The letter has disappeared and Buck only summarised the contents, but he is clear that Elizabeth, 'being very desirous to be married, and growing not only impatient of delays', asked Howard 'to be a mediator for her in the cause of the marriage to the king, who, as she wrote, was her only joy and maker in this world, and that she was his in heart and in thoughts, in body, and in all'.[26] It has been suggested that Elizabeth's real purpose was only to ask Howard to remind the King that he had promised to find her a suitable husband, and that Buck has misconstrued her meaning;[27] but hints of a close relationship between Richard and his niece also exist in two books owned by him in which Elizabeth inscribed her name. One is a partial copy of the French prose *Tristan* in which she wrote 'sans re[mo]vyr Elyzabeth' (without changing, Elizabeth), and the other a verse translation of Boethius's *De consolatione philosophiae* in French to which she added her signature and, interestingly, her uncle's motto *loyalte me lye*. The Princess usually signed herself 'Elizabeth, the King's daughter' or (later) 'Elizabeth the Queen', but could use neither style in the period between her father's death in April 1483 and her marriage to Henry VII in January 1486. Both inscriptions can therefore be dated to Richard's reign (she is unlikely to have used his motto in the five months that elapsed between his death and her marriage), and it may be assumed that she borrowed the books from him or that he gave them to her as tokens of his regard.[28]

Queen Anne's death on 16 March made a marriage between Richard and Elizabeth even more likely, but the scheme faltered because two of his councillors, Sir Richard Ratcliffe and William Catesby, told him bluntly, 'to his face', as the Croyland chronicler has it, that his loyal notherners would rise against him if he attempted to 'gratify an incestuous passion for his said niece'.[29] Their real concern was that a new Woodville queen would seek to punish them for their part in the executions of Earl Rivers and Lord Richard Grey; but Richard was so beholden to them that, before the month was out, he stood before the mayor and citizens of London in the great hall of the Knights of St John at Clerkenwell and declared publicly that the possibility of marrying his niece had never occurred to him! Elizabeth Woodville knew differently, however, and had probably thought long and hard before approving a plan that would make her daughter queen (and a future grandson king), but would deny the throne to her surviving son.

Another problem that would have confronted King Richard if the matter had proceeded was that he could not repeal the Act of Parliament that had bastardised his niece without also relegitimising her sisters and her surviving brother. He would have been obliged to concede that the grounds on which he had deposed Edward V were invalid, and that Prince Richard was, *ipso facto*, the rightful heir. Commentators have argued that this proves that the boy was already dead and that the King knew it; but it is by no means the only possible explanation. Elizabeth Woodville would have realised that the proposed marriage placed her son in renewed danger (however much Richard sought to mollify her), and may have suggested that he should 'disappear' even more thoroughly than when he was lodged with trusted courtiers. The *Parallel* says that Richard of Eastwell was delivered into the care of a Latin schoolmaster (presumably a clergyman) at Lutterworth, in south Leicestershire, and it is curious that the Greys of Groby, Elizabeth's first husband's family, held the manor and advowson of Lutterworth and presented rectors from 1459/60 to 1523. This quiet place, situated just off the Watling Street and approximately 16 miles from Leicester, would have seemed a suitable abode for a boy who was to live in obscurity but whose future was to be carefully monitored. It was well away from the centres of government but could be reached quickly if the need arose.

The rector in 1485 was one John Varnam, a canon and prebendary of South Grantham in Salisbury Cathedral who had been appointed to Lutterworth in 1476/7 and who held the post until he was succeeded by Master John Lane (otherwise Lawne) on 5 August 1486. He would have been known to Queen Elizabeth and her son Thomas, Marquess Dorset (who had become Lord Ferrers (Grey) of Groby on the death of his grandmother two years earlier), and had previously been granted joint custody of most of the lands of Sir William Trussel of Elmesthorpe in Leicestershire (d. 1480) during the minority of Trussel's son and heir Edward.[30] Edward may not have lived in Varnam's household; but the implication is that those in authority thought him a suitable person to look after a young man's interests. Again, we cannot expect to find written proof of something that, even then, was a closely guarded secret; but Varnam had all the right 'credentials', and it would have been a simple matter to take Prince Richard (a.k.a. Richard of Eastwell) from Lutterworth to Bosworth the day before the battle. His uncle, who did not expect to remarry or beget a son in the immediate future, could have begun to think more seriously about the merits of the vague prospect he had dangled before the Queen-dowager, and may have hoped that recognising Edward IV's son as his successor at this moment would persuade more of his late brother's supporters who had joined the opposition to come to terms with him and seal his victory. But the Prince became not the heir to the throne but a fugitive – and the question, of course, is what happened to him then?

# SIX

# *The Colchester 'Connection'*

Richard Plantagenet of Eastwell and Prince Richard of York have hitherto been regarded as two separate, distinct persons, but there is reason to suppose that they were actually one and the same. In the first place there is no evidence that Richard of Eastwell existed before 1483 (except for the stories recounted by Dr Brett and others in the eighteenth century), and no proof that Richard of York was alive after this date. There is, as we have noted, no reason why a third illegitimate child of Richard III should have been hidden when his siblings were provided for, and every reason why a son of Edward IV would choose to live incognito rather than be seen to pose a threat to the new, Tudor, government. He could have made a bid for the throne – like Perkin Warbeck, for example – but Warbeck's career had ended on the gallows, and it is likely that Richard's friends' prime consideration was to preserve his life.

How, then, was this accomplished, and what can we discern of Richard as he grew to manhood in the closing years of the fifteenth century? The later sources do not identify the 'gentleman' who paid his board and took him to Bosworth, but the most likely candidate is Francis, Viscount Lovel, King

Autograph of Francis, Viscount Lovel.

Richard's chamberlain and closest friend. The Lovels were an old armigerous family who had recently built a fine new manor house at Minster Lovel in Oxfordshire, and it is likely that Francis was born there, probably in November 1456. He was heir to no fewer than five baronies, the lordships of Lovel, Holand and Burnell held by his father John (a former Lancastrian who had made his peace with King Edward), together with Deincourt and Grey of Rotherfield, which he would acquire on the death of his grandmother Lady Alice. Richard and Francis may have first encountered each other at Middleham Castle in Yorkshire when, as boys, their knightly training was entrusted to the Earl of Warwick; but Richard was some four years older and may have left Middleham before Lovel arrived. Francis became the ward of the Duke of Suffolk after Warwick was slain at the battle of Barnet, but he had been married in childhood to Anne Fitzhugh, daughter of Henry, Lord Fitzhugh of Ravensworth (Yorks.), the 'Kingmaker's' brother-in-law, and may have increasingly thought of northern England as 'home'. He would certainly have come to know Richard of Gloucester, who in the interval had become King Edward's 'Lord of the North', at some time before or after he attained his majority in 1477, and they had become comrades in arms by the time Richard led an army into Scotland in 1481. He undoubtedly had many contacts (and possible refuges) in northern England together with others in his native Oxfordshire; but in the immediate aftermath of Bosworth he turned his horse eastwards and galloped nearly 200 miles to St John's Abbey at Colchester.[1] He was accompanied by Humphrey and Thomas Stafford of Grafton (Worcs.), two other reliable royal lieutenants, and they appear to have remained there in sanctuary for the next few months.

Fifteenth-century Colchester was a vibrant, prosperous community of some 4,000 people who had enjoyed local self-government since Richard I had granted them a charter in 1189. Their wealth was based on the cloth trade – Colchester 'grey' was sold in Toulouse and Gascony – but agriculture was still important and many profited from the oyster fishery on the River Colne. They were largely self-sufficient – some of the men met local needs by working as artisans and shopkeepers, while their wives brewed the ale that slaked the thirst of the visitors to the two great annual fairs. The midsummer fair held on St John's Green and the St Denis fair that came round in October attracted visitors from all over Essex, and were two of the high points of their social and commercial year. Professor Martin suggests that they were Yorkist in sympathy during the Wars of the Roses, but their main concern was perhaps rather to avoid disruption. They accepted a new charter from Edward IV much as they had received another granted them by his Lancastrian rival Henry VI a few years earlier – with gratitude but with a willingness to accommodate themselves to the powers that be.

The town was dominated by its Norman castle (used as the county gaol from the thirteenth century onwards), and by the eight churches that stood within its walls. At least five of these were enlarged in the fourteenth and fifteenth centuries, and came to incorporate no fewer than ten chantries (established by affluent townsmen), besides many lesser endowments for prayers and almsgiving. The Benedictines of St John's were only one of four resident religious orders. The Augustinian canons had been established at St Botolph's priory since 1110, and there were houses of Franciscan and Crouched friars. A grammar school, which prepared boys for the universities and the Church, had existed for several centuries, and would soon be complemented by an 'academy' where apprentices who had completed their basic schooling could be trained in commercial subjects. The Black Death had done its deadly work here as in other places, but there was very much an air of revival by 1485.[2]

St John's Abbey had been founded by Eudo Dapifer (steward), the Norman constable of Colchester Castle, on the site of a small wooden church consecrated to St John the Evangelist that had a reputation for miracles. The abbey church burned down in 1133, but was rebuilt on a scale that reflected its growing wealth and influence. Five pinnacles surmounted the massive central tower (a great one in the centre and a lesser at each corner), and two castellated towers flanked the decorated west front. By the late fifteenth century the abbey was patron of, and appointed clergy to, no fewer than six parish churches (two within the walls and four without), and one of the monks usually served as curate of another, St Giles's, which had been a chapel in the monastic cemetery. The abbot was mitred, which meant that he was entitled to attend Parliament, but he was not always popular with the local townspeople. His legal jurisdiction over the tenants who farmed the abbey's lands within the town, and the abbey's right of chartered sanctuary, led to frequent disputes with the borough, and the King had formally defined (that is, limited) the bounds of the sanctuary as recently as 13 May 1453. There were twenty-six monks in 1465, and probably a similar number when Lovel and the Stafford brothers rode through the great gatehouse (now the only surviving part of the abbey) in August 1485.[3]

The abbot was Walter Stansted, who had been appointed in 1468 and who held the position until his death in 1497. He was not a noted Yorkist or Ricardian – neither King Edward nor King Richard had rewarded him or showed him particular favour – but his house was regarded as a safe haven by Yorkist

St John's Abbey Gate, Colchester (from Philip Morant, *The History and Antiquities of the Most Ancient Town and Borough of Colchester* (1748), facing p. 36).

dissidents. In 1489 Abbot John Sante of Abingdon and others were attainted for their part in an unsuccessful conspiracy to overthrow Henry VII and liberate Edward, Earl of Warwick (the executed Duke of Clarence's son), from the Tower of London. Their vague, almost farcical, plan involved writing a letter that would be left near the Earl's room as though it had been accidentally dropped by an unknown well-wisher. It was to be addressed to 'some good felowe' (presumably the person who was meant to find it or a name that would identify the intended recipient), telling Warwick to join them *in Colchester*, after he had escaped.[4] Much the same thing happened ten years later when Robert Cleymound, who had become the Earl's keeper in the Tower, joined a group of plotters who hoped to free both Warwick and the pretender Perkin Warbeck and make one of them (it is not clear which one) king. Cleymound may have been a double agent who secretly informed on his co-conspirators (he was never, apparently, tried or punished after the plot was 'discovered'), and went out of his way to avoid arousing their suspicions.[5] Thomas Ward, another member of the group, was unconvinced when Cleymound tried to gain his confidence by telling him that he thought some of their plans were already known to King Henry; but their exchange is interesting because Cleymound told Ward that he was going to seek sanctuary *in Colchester*, while he still could. He did not go, of course, but the implication was clearly that, if he had genuinely feared for his safety, Colchester, 60 miles from London, would have been his preferred place of refuge. Nearby Westminster, which had sheltered Queen Elizabeth Woodville, was a more obvious safe haven (indeed, Ward even suggested it to him), but Cleymound's mind was already made up.

We do not know the nature of Sante and Cleymound's previous contacts with St John's Abbey, but Francis Lovel would have known Abbot Stansted personally. They almost certainly encountered one another in the early 1470s after Lovel became the ward of the Duke of Suffolk, and would have met subsequently on great state occasions both before, and after, he attained his majority. They may, or may not, have been present at King Edward's reburial of his father Richard, Duke of York, at Fotheringhay (Northants.) in July, 1476, and it is unclear if they both attended Prince Richard's marriage to Anne Mowbray eighteen months later; but they almost certainly renewed their acquaintanceship at Richard III's coronation in

July 1483 (where Lovel bore the third sword and provided for the Queen's ring), and both were summoned to attend Parliament on 9 December the same year.[6]

It is possible to speculate that Lovel and Stansted may have become friends as a result of these encounters, but this alone would not have justified Lovel's long journey after Bosworth. He may have thought Colchester a convenient place from which to escape to Burgundy (an idea which could also have influenced Abbot Sante and Robert Cleymound), but there were other, nearer, escape routes and Lovel did not, in any case, go abroad for the present. Early in 1486 he rode to Middleham in north Yorkshire where he stirred up an insurrection and tried unsuccessfully to capture Henry VII in York towards the end of April. He then sought refuge with Sir Thomas Broughton, another Yorkist dissident, at his house in Broughton in Furness on the coast of Lancashire, before making his way to the Isle of Ely and joining the new Lambert Simnel conspiracy being fomented in Oxford.[7] The Stafford brothers also left St John's either with or at about the same time as Lovel, and made for the west country from where they plotted to seize Worcester. Their journey to Colchester had therefore been equally pointless – unless, of course, they had all been entrusted with a particular mission which obliged them to go there before considering any other course of action. King Richard may have thought Lutterworth too precarious a refuge for his nephew if Henry Tudor gained the victory, and ordered Lovel and the Staffords to deliver the boy into the safer hands of Abbot Stansted in the event of his defeat or death.

Our theory then is based on the following considerations:

1. St John's Abbey at Colchester was widely regarded by dissident Yorkists as a safe refuge.
2. Lovel and the Stafford brothers had no reason to go there in August 1485 unless they had a particular, secret purpose.

3. Richard III would have had little hesitation in choosing Lovel, the last surviving member of the 'cat, rat and dog' triumvirate, and the devoted Staffords, to fulfil this confidential undertaking if the worst happened.

This may indeed be why Lovel and Humphrey and Thomas Stafford were neither killed nor captured at Bosworth when so many other close associates of King Richard either fell into the hands of the victors or died in his last desperate charge against his enemies. They may have watched the battle from a safe distance in young Richard's company before turning their horses eastwards towards Colchester, which they would have reached almost a week later. Abbot Stansted doubtless had a number of boys in his house already, and could receive another without anyone's suspicions being aroused.

Henry Tudor may have known that Prince Richard was still alive even before he set out on his expedition to Bosworth, and would have lost no time in ascertaining his whereabouts after he became king. The boy could have shared the fate of the young Earl of Warwick – imprisonment in the Tower and, eventually, execution – but this would not have been acceptable to the Woodvilles or other friends of his father. Henry's problem was that nullifying Richard III's *Titulus Regius* (the Act that had declared Edward IV's marriage invalid and his children bastards) would legitimate not only Princess Elizabeth of York (whom he had promised to marry), but also her younger brother. Prince Richard had a better claim to the throne than Henry, and would pose an obvious threat if his survival became public knowledge; but how could the King neutralise him without revealing his existence or damaging his own relations with his Yorkist allies? One way was to enter into an agreement with the two Elizabeths (his wife-to-be and his future mother-in-law) that Richard would be allowed to live at St John's unmolested on condition that he was given a completely new persona and effectively isolated from politics. It was not an ideal solution, for Richard, for Henry, or for the Woodvilles; but it was better than more conflict or seriously jeopardising the child's life.

It is interesting that, although Lovel and the Stafford brothers remained at Colchester for approximately six months after their flight from Bosworth (far beyond the forty days that sanctuary men were given to choose between surrendering to the royal justice and exile), Henry made no attempt to seize them or make their lives more difficult. Instead he opened discussions with them, and before long was confident that he had reached an understanding that would allow them to endorse the arrangements made with the two Elizabeths. Many years later Sir Hugh Conway recounted how he had passed on reliable information that Lovel intended to leave Colchester and continue the struggle, but that the King had refused to believe it. Henry 'said that hyt could not be so, and resoned with me always to the contrary of my said sayyngs'.[8] Henry would not have thought this of one of Richard III's staunchest supporters unless he had good reason, and must have supposed that Lovel would see that his own future – and that of his young charge – depended upon his cooperating with the new Tudor government. William Catesby, the 'cat' of the rhyme, was also in no doubt that Francis would 'come to grace' (as his will, made shortly before his execution three days after Bosworth, puts it[9]), probably because he too believed that Prince Richard's safety would transcend all else.

It is clear that Richard's fate would have rested, ultimately, with King Henry, so did taking him to Colchester really achieve anything? The answer is yes to the extent that it ensured that he was not killed in the rout after Bosworth (unlike Prince Edward of Lancaster, who had been slain in the heat of the moment at Tewkesbury), and to the extent that Henry also seems to have trusted Abbot Stansted and decided to 'adopt' Richard III's arrangements. The boy was not to be an English 'Man in the Iron Mask', but he was to be kept both securely and obscurely, with his identity known to as few people as possible. Lovel had presumably calculated that he could continue to resist Henry without involving – and therefore endangering – him, and this may be why the pretender Lambert Simnel was trained to impersonate the young Earl of Warwick. But there was always a possibility that the King would decide that all these trails led ultimately to Richard, and no uprising could be entirely without risk.

If all this is true, we would expect to find Henry keeping a close, watchful eye on St John's, especially during the first, uncertain, years of his government, and there is evidence that this was indeed the case. In June/July 1486, Philip Knighton, one of four 'messengers of the Exchequer', was sent to Colchester 'with secret letters from the king's council'.[10] This was shortly after Henry had returned to London following the collapse of the uprisings led by Lovel and the Stafford brothers, a moment when, perhaps for the first time in his brief but so far hectic reign, he could pause to take stock of the situation. We can only conjecture that Prince Richard was the subject of these letters, but clearly there was a secret matter that concerned both Colchester and the King.

Henry also visited Colchester himself regularly, particularly in the period before and after the Lambert Simnel rebellion. He sealed documents there in the course of his 'progress' around East Anglia on 2 and 10 April 1487, included the town in his March 1489 tour of the region, and was back again on 19/20 July 1491.[11] He did not, apparently, visit other comparable towns – Great Yarmouth, for example – as frequently, if ever, and the implication is again that Colchester was of particular interest or concern to him. As late as 1515 Catherine of Aragon, Henry VIII's queen, 'passed through Colchester on a pilgrimage to the shrine at Walsingham in Norfolk', and was escorted to St John's by the town's bailiffs, who went out to meet her on the London road.[12] Her father-in-law had concluded his 1493 progress with a similar visit, but Catherine had no need to travel via Colchester unless she had a particular reason. She would normally have followed the road from London east as far as Chelmsford and then turned northwards passing through Sudbury, Bury St Edmunds, Thetford, Swaffham and on towards Fakenham (the route of the modern A131, A134 and A1065). Visiting Colchester meant travelling another 24 miles to the east (the best part of a day's riding) before looking towards Walsingham, and it is possible that she wanted to see for herself how a potential rival for her husband's throne had been neutralised. Richard would have been 42 by now, and no longer a 'kingly' figure, but more of this anon.

Colchester was also home to a lady named Eleanor Kechyn (Kitchen), who was pardoned for unspecified offences on 5 February 1491. The grant is printed in the *Calendar of the Patent Rolls*, and is worth quoting in full:

> General pardon to Eleanor Kechyn, *alias* Kechen, *alias* Kechyne, late of Colchester, co. Essex, widow, *alias* 'huswyf', for offences before 18 December last, provided that she find security not to go at large during the rest of her life, but remain in the custody of her parents or nearest kinfolks.[13]

Eleanor had clearly offended the Crown in some way or she would not have needed a royal pardon, but the conditions attached to it were quite remarkable. She had to promise and find sureties that she would not 'go at large *for the rest of her life*' (emphasis added), and that she would live with her parents, and after their deaths with her 'nearest kinfolks'. Any prospect of remarriage was apparently to be denied her, and she was to be supervised by members of her own family in what can only be described as a state of perpetual house imprisonment. This does not suggest that she had committed some minor, everyday felony – rather, that it was altogether something more serious – and we can only wonder if she was made subject to these restrictions because she had acquired some knowledge or information which touched the King personally and which she was to be given no opportunity to gossip abroad.

It is not improbable that Eleanor had been married as a young girl to a much older husband, rather like the young wife of the Paris Ménagier (so brilliantly brought to life by Eileen Power), or wise Thomas Betson's juvenile fiancée Katherine Ryche.[14] She was still young herself in 1491 (or it is unlikely that both her parents would still have been living), but her presumed spouse, Thomas Kechyn, had been admitted as a free burgess of Colchester many years earlier in 1467/8.[15] Very little more is known about her, but at some time before her confinement she crossed swords with Mark Walker, a London grocer, who claimed that her late husband had owed him £14 10s. Walker 'afermed in the seid cite of London afore the maier and aldermen of the same cite age[nst the] seid Elianore as Executrix of the tastament of the seid Thom[a]s hir husbond a pleynt of dette of xiiij li. x s. upon a concessit solvere that shuld abe [have been] made by the seid [Thomas] hir husbond to the seid Mark', and Eleanor asked the Archbishop of Canterbury to grant a 'writte of cerciorari' (certiorari), which she hoped would save her from further harassment. Walker was, she said, 'a dweller and a man of great myght power and knowlegge w[ith]ine the seid cite and your poore Bedwoman a stranger he intending utt[er]ly by his great myght and power w[ith]ine the seid cite to recov[er]e the seid xiiij li. x s. of yo[ur] seid Bedwoman agenst all right and good conciens'. Her case was that her husband had repaid Walker prior to his death 'as it apperith in writynges of the seid Mark', and moreover that she had never been appointed his executrix.[16] The mistake may have been genuine, but high-handedness and sharp practice could taint merchants and businessmen as well as lords.

A writ of certiorari was a common-law prerogative writ issued by an appellate court requiring a lower court to deliver a case record for judicial review,[17] but we do not know if the Archbishop responded in the way Eleanor wished. No writ apparently survives for her, and it is impossible to know which court (if any) was asked to examine the subject of her petition. There were several provincial courts of the Archbishops of Canterbury, but no records survive for the Archbishop's Court of Audience for this period and there is apparently nothing of interest in the archives of the Prerogative Court of Canterbury, which normally dealt with testamentary business. Eleanor appealed to the Archbishop as Lord Chancellor of England (that is, to the Court of Chancery), but there is nothing to indicate which of the courts at Westminster, Chancery, King's Bench, Common Pleas or Star Chamber might have dealt with her alleged 'offences'. If Thomas Kechyn had left a will in the Prerogative Court of Canterbury, a 'sentence' would have been entered into the wills' register as a result of his testament being disputed, but, unfortunately, he did not.[18]

The Archbishop who received Eleanor's appeal was our old friend John Morton, and it is possible that he became aware of other, potentially more serious, matters while her dispute with Walker was being examined. Prince Richard would have been 17 in 1490, easily old enough to succumb to the charms of a young widow, and the possibility that he might secretly marry her and sire children would have rung alarm bells all over Westminster. The only solution would be to separate them and ensure that they remained separated, a decision that would explain Eleanor's curious pardon and accompanying 'sentence'. Abbot Stansted doubtless received a terse letter from Morton telling him that Richard had been allowed too much licence and must be kept closer until he was satisfied that the danger had passed.

So is this what really happened or are we allowing imagination to run away with us? It is, of course, possible that Francis Lovel's long, apparently unnecessary journey to Colchester, the secret letters carried by Philip Knighton, King Henry's frequent visits, and the strange fate of Eleanor Kitchen may be no more than unrelated coincidences, but it seems that something was causing concern there in the last years of the fifteenth century and the first part of the next. What that *something* was is never indicated and we can only assume that it concerned Prince Richard – but it was clearly a sensitive matter, too sensitive to be mentioned even in official documents. Henry VII spent the entire twenty-four years of his reign denying any knowledge of the fate of the Princes (except, of course, when he published Tyrell's implausible confession), and the implication is that he did know but could not say. If the boys were dead, he could have blamed nature, blamed Richard III, blamed Buckingham, blamed anyone; but if one of them was alive, there was no one to blame for murdering him and all enquiries and speculations would be officially discouraged. This seems to have been the situation – and, while it does not in any way prove our theory, it is entirely consistent with the known facts.

# SEVEN

# *In the Shadows*

Prince Richard disappears from the record in 1483, but this does not, of course, prove that he had died. Commentators writing at a distance or without access to the court usually made this assumption (see Chapter One), but those better informed were more cautious. The Croyland chronicler only mentions a rumour – he does not say that the Princes were dead, as he might well have done if he knew they had been murdered – and Sir William Stanley's alleged remark that, 'if he were sure that the man [Perkin Warbeck] was [King] Edward's son, he would never take up arms against him'[1] reflects the continuing uncertainty. Stanley, Henry VII's chamberlain and the younger brother of Lord Thomas, the King's mother's husband, was well placed to learn what had happened to the Princes, and was apparently prepared to believe that Prince Richard was still living in 1495. It is usually assumed that he had no particular knowledge and was prepared to take Warbeck at face value; but it is possible to read his words as a definitive statement that one of King Edward's sons had survived – the only uncertainty was whether Perkin was the young man in question. Polydore Vergil did not have to mention this story in his authorised history, and we can only wonder if it was another hint to his readers that his account of their deaths (their murder by Tyrell) was not really true.

The arrangements made for Prince Richard at Colchester were an official, state secret, but it was arguably a secret known to too many people for Henry VII to feel entirely safe or comfortable. He would have shared it with those he could trust, his mother, Margaret Beaufort, her husband, Lord Stanley, Abbot Stansted (who, unlike M. de Saint-Mars, the 'Mask's' gaoler, would have known the identity of his 'prisoner') and intimate councillors like John Morton, Giles Daubeney, Richard Fox, Reginald Bray and Thomas Lovell; but had to accept that there were others – friends and enemies – who had learned of it before he became king. There was Francis Lovel, the Stafford brothers and Abbot Sante, of course, and Queen Elizabeth Woodville and her immediate family, her five daughters (including Henry's wife Elizabeth) and Dorset, her eldest son. It would have been difficult to keep the matter from the boy's aunts, Margaret of Burgundy and Elizabeth of Suffolk, and if the latter knew so too did her husband, the Duke, and her sons, John, Edmund and Richard, who would all arguably seek the Crown for themselves. Then there were those court officials who had served Edward IV and who were restored to positions of influence by Henry, men like Oliver King, the late King's secretary, who became bishop of Bath and Wells, Prince Richard's attorney Andrew Dymock, who became Henry's solicitor, and Piers Curteys, who was reappointed keeper of the privy palace of Westminster and of the Great Wardrobe. Their knowledge may have influenced some of their actions, and may explain why the Dean of St Paul's, William Worsley, a substantial landowner in Essex, was prepared to risk everything to help Perkin Warbeck. Some of these were dead by the end of the fifteenth century, and few survived beyond the first decade of the next; but Henry can never have been certain precisely who did, or did not, know.

The Yorkist dissidents' best chance of deposing Henry came early in 1487, when what is usually known as the Lambert Simnel rebellion was fomented, first in Oxford and then in Ireland. Vergil tells us that Simnel, the young, personable son of an Oxford tradesman, was taught courtly manners by an ambitious local priest, Richard Simons, 'so that if ever he should pretend the lad to be of royal descent (as he had planned to do) people would the more readily believe it and have absolute trust in his bold deceit'.[2] Simons took the boy to Dublin, where he 'secretly summoned a meeting of a considerable number of Irish nobles' and convinced them that his protégé was Edward, Earl of Warwick, the Yorkist heir-apparent, who had been imprisoned in the Tower since Bosworth. The House of York had always been popular in Ireland, but this does not explain why the Irish peers responded so readily to someone who was socially of little consequence or how Simons was able to deceive them. The only logical explanation is that others with greater knowledge and experience had been involved in training Simnel, and that the Irish nobles had agreed to make him the focus of an uprising against Henry even before he and his mentor set foot in the country. The King's only consolation was that his enemies – even those who had so far cooperated with his government – would now have little alternative but to declare themselves or, at the very least, risk being found out.

The rebels engaged the support of Margaret of Burgundy, who provided them with a force of German and Swiss mercenaries commanded by Martin Schwarz, a redoubtable soldier. Schwarz and his men arrived in Dublin in time to witness Simnel's 'coronation' as 'Edward VI' on 24 May 1487, and the combined army sailed for England at the beginning of June. Once disembarked, they marched rapidly, hoping to force a battle before the royal army had fully mustered, but found the country largely hostile or indifferent to them. A few who were diehard Yorkists or had quarrels to settle with Tudor sympathisers brought soldiers or gave supplies or money, but the force that confronted Henry at Stoke, 4 miles south of Newark, on 16 June was inferior to the royalists in both numbers and equipment. A battle of some three hours' duration culminated in the defeat of the rebels and the deaths of most of their leaders. Simnel and Simons were captured, the former becoming a scullion in the royal kitchens (he was clearly an innocent who had been 'used' by others), while the latter disappeared into an ecclesiastical prison. Henry emerged strengthened from this challenge to his authority, but it was not an experience he would wish to repeat.

Francis Lovel joined the Simnel conspiracy in its early stages, crossed to Burgundy to encourage Duchess Margaret, and subsequently fought for the Yorkists at the battle of Stoke. He was thought to have escaped from the conflict, but his friend, Edward Frank, was unable to find him in northern England and he did not, apparently, take advantage of a safe conduct that would have allowed him to enter Scotland.[3] Lord Bacon's biography of Henry VII mentioned a rumour that 'he lived long after in a cave or vault',[4] and this seemed to be confirmed when a male skeleton was discovered in a concealed chamber at Minster Lovel, his Oxfordshire manor house, in 1708. The remains were found 'as having been sitting at a table',[5] suggesting that the victim, whoever he was, had died suddenly and without warning, and it is possible to speculate that, although Lovel had sought refuge with his former tenants and servants, they had been able to protect him for only a few weeks or months. I have argued elsewhere that Henry hoped to learn more about the Simnel conspiracy from Lovel and may even have been ready to pardon him;[6] but he was a dangerous adversary who knew a potentially devastating secret. He may have perished because something happened to the servant who held the key to his prison (as some modern writers have suggested), but it is not impossible that royal agents learned of his whereabouts and silenced him before he could cause Henry more trouble.

The failure of Lovel's earlier 1486 uprising had precipitated the collapse of the Stafford brothers' rebellion in Worcestershire, and they had sought refuge in the Abbot of Abingdon's sanctuary of Culham. Culham should have been as safe as St John's, but they were forcibly removed after only two days and Humphrey brought to trial on 20 June. He argued that the officers who had taken them had acted illegally and that he should be returned to the sanctuary, but the royal justices were having none of it. They adjourned the case while they summoned Abbot Sante to show evidence of the rights he claimed for his property, but they knew the King wanted a conviction and obliged him by ruling that sanctuary could not be pleaded in cases of treason.[7] This sealed Humphrey's fate, and he was executed shortly after 5 July, but Thomas, his brother, was not tried and, in Vergil's phrase, 'earned a pardon'.[8] Edward Hall tells us that this was 'because he was thought not to have done it of his own will and malicious mind but through the evil counsel and persuasion of his elder brother',[9] but was Henry moved by considerations other than mere kindness? Would it be stretching credibility too far to suggest that Humphrey had agreed to say nothing untoward in his last speech from the scaffold, and that Thomas was granted his life in return for this and his own silence? In any case, Thomas disappears from history (which may imply that he remained in prison or at least avoided all political involvement thereafter), and took what he knew of Prince Richard to his grave.

Abbot John Sante, Lovel's friend and the Staffords' protector, must also have known the reason for their journey to Colchester. He was a lifelong Yorkist who had served Edward IV as an ambassador and taken a prominent part in the King's funeral obsequies, but old loyalties alone would not have justified his continuing opposition to the new government. He behaved more circumspectly after Humphrey's execution and in March 1488 was appointed to help negotiate a treaty between the King of France and the Duke of Brittany. But he had not changed his political opinions and was attainted after his wrong-headed plan to liberate the Earl of Warwick from the Tower was discovered the following year. He was pardoned on 2 February 1493 on condition that a mass for King Henry was celebrated every day in his abbey, but may have died shortly afterwards.[10] His efforts to free Warwick could imply that he hoped to crown him in place of Henry Tudor, but the young Earl was the Kingmaker's grandson and would be a key player in any plan to make Richard of York king.

Two others who were involved with Lovel, and who almost certainly played some part in instigating the Simnel conspiracy against Henry, were the Bishop of Bath and Wells, Robert Stillington, and the queen-dowager, Elizabeth Woodville. Stillington, who served Edward IV as chancellor from 1467 to 1470 and again from 1471 to 1473, was a career civil servant who seldom visited his diocese. His knowledge of Edward's pre-contract had been used to justify Richard III's accession, and Henry VII ordered his arrest the day after Bosworth. The King's agents brought him to York in great distress 'sore crased by reason of his trouble', and were persuaded by the mayor, Nicholas Lancaster, to allow him to 'continue still within the said citie for iv. or v. days for his ease and rest'.[11] He pleaded 'his grete age, long infirmite and feblenes',[12] when he successfully petitioned for a pardon in November, and then made his way to Oxford, where he met Lovel and the other plotters. Henry again ordered his arrest in March 1487, but he took refuge in the University and refused to surrender. The masters tried to protect him – they argued that they could not, in conscience, compel him to yield to the King's agents – but the threat of force and the loss of their franchises appears to have changed their minds.[13] He was taken to Windsor and spent some time in custody before being allowed to retire to his episcopal manor of Dogmersfield, where he died in 1491.[14] It would have been ironic if someone who had contributed so much to Edward V's downfall had now contemplated restoring his younger brother, but the world had altered significantly since Richard had gained the kingdom and Henry clearly 'thought him a dangerous man'.[15]

Elizabeth Woodville's part in the uprising is more problematic, since her involvement was never formally admitted by the government; but in February 1487 she was deprived of all her property and sent to spend the rest of her life at Bermondsey Abbey. Polydore Vergil admits that she was being punished, but says it was because she had risked damaging Henry's prospects by surrendering her daughters to King Richard three years earlier. He ignores the very real difficulties that had confronted her during her months in sanctuary, difficulties that Henry evidently appreciated when he restored her to her dignity as queen-dowager after Bosworth, and does not explain why the King – who had nevertheless married her daughter and become a father – decided to punish her for an 'offence' that had made no difference to him. It is clear from the other decisions taken at the meeting of the Council that deprived Elizabeth – decisions to offer pardon to all offenders and to allow the real Earl of Warwick to be seen in public – that the government was really concerned with the new conspiracy, and Lord Bacon commented that the queen-dowager was so tainted with treason that 'it was almost thought dangerous to visit her, or see her'.[16] Henry's problem was that he could not charge his mother-in-law – still less put her on trial – without alienating other members of her family and proclaiming the weakness of his dynasty to the courts of Europe. The result was that she was consigned to the political wilderness (by being placed in what may be termed 'secure accommodation'), and her offences were said to have been committed before Henry became king.

Some writers have rejected this theory, arguing that Elizabeth 'retired' to Bermondsey and surrendered her lands as part of an amicable family settlement, but aristocratic ladies did not usually forgo wealth and influence without good reason.[17] Objections that Henry continued to refer to her in endearing terms and even thought of marrying her to the King of Scots can be dismissed without difficulty,[18] but would she have sought to depose her own daughter to deliver the crown to the son of her old enemy, the Duke of Clarence? I have argued elsewhere that Queen Elizabeth of York could have been married to the Earl of Warwick after Henry had been vanquished (a union that would have made Elizabeth Woodville the real power behind the inexperienced young couple's throne), but how much easier to explain her involvement in the Simnel uprising if she knew that Prince Richard was still living. The rebellion had been organised on behalf of Warwick, and the 'feigned boy' claimed to be Warwick; but he would fall away naturally if an undoubted son of Edward IV emerged from the shadows after the Yorkists had triumphed. But the enterprise ended disastrously, and Elizabeth lost all hope of ever seeing Richard again.

Richard was still a child, malleable enough to adapt to his new life at Colchester, and may have found the 'normality' of his situation a welcome change from the rigours of court protocol. We do not know how much he was told or discovered – whether he learned of the Simnel uprising or understood its possible implications – or how he felt when the news of his mother's death reached him in 1492. He was almost 19 by then and presumably had had no contact with her for more than seven years; but he must sometimes have thought of his five sisters and they of him. It is not impossible that some of them tried to maintain contact with him through intermediaries (where their own circumstances permitted it), and perhaps occasionally to send him small gifts or tokens of affection. This would hardly have been possible for the two youngest, Bridget, who became a nun at Dartford, and Catherine, who was married to William Courteney in distant Devon; but Anne, who married Thomas Howard, afterwards Duke of Norfolk, Cecily, who enjoyed the friendship of Henry's mother, Lady Margaret Beaufort, and Henry's wife, Elizabeth, would all have had better opportunities. Anne was nearest to Colchester geographically, but perhaps Cecily and Elizabeth felt more protective towards their 'little' brother and tried to help him when they could.

Cecily was placed in the custody of the Lady Margaret in September 1485, and her marriage to Ralph Scrope, a supporter of Richard III, was dissolved the next year. She married John, Viscount Welles, Margaret's half-brother, late in 1487, and enjoyed an amicable relationship with the new royal family until Welles died in 1498. She then wed a lowly esquire, Thomas Kyme of Friskney (Lincs.), without asking the King's permission, and it was again Lady Margaret who sheltered them both at her house at Collyweston (Northants.) while she tried to assuage her son's anger and mitigate the financial penalties. It was thanks to her that Cecily was allowed to keep some of the Welles estates for life, and that she and Kyme avoided the fines that would normally have been imposed for marrying and occupying the lands without royal consent. She was undoubtedly close to Margaret, and this could have helped her to assist Richard; but Margaret's prime concern was always for Henry, and she probably ensured that the 'arrangement' was rigidly enforced. All we can say is that nothing seems to have clouded or eroded their friendship, and Margaret paid some of Cecily's funeral expenses when she died in 1507.[19]

Queen Elizabeth of York should have been still better placed to help her younger brother, but her marriage to Henry was first and foremost a political union, which allowed her very little scope or influence. Henry had promised to marry her to secure Yorkist backing when he had been an exile with few prospects; and it may have been partly to emphasise that he was king as of right (and not in right of his wife) that he delayed solemnising their marriage until January 1486 and did not allow her to be crowned until November 1487. Elizabeth remained in the shadows, the bearer of the royal children (Ayala, the Spanish ambassador, wrote that she was 'beloved, because she is powerless'[20]), and would have been careful not wilfully to offend her husband or his all-powerful mother. Her privy purse accounts survive for 1502–3, the last year of her life, but no horseman was paid to ride to Colchester and no amounts of money disbursed for obscure purposes.[21] Prince Richard would by then have been almost 30, and perhaps so much part of his new life and environment that attempts to contact him would have been scarcely worth the risk.

King Henry could dominate these royal ladies either through his immediate family or through their husbands, but their half-brother Thomas Grey, Marquess of Dorset, was an altogether different matter. Dorset must have known that Prince Richard was still living, and Henry not only prevented him from abandoning his little court in exile in 1484 but was apparently cautious – some might say apprehensive – of him thereafter. He was one of two noblemen left behind in France as security for the repayment of moneys loaned when Henry set out on his 'victorious journey'; and, although he tried to approach the King in East Anglia when the Simnel rebellion threatened 'to purge himself of some accusations which had been made against him', Henry declined to speak with him. Bacon says that the King 'kept an ear for him' (that is, was prepared to give him a fair hearing on another occasion), but instructed the Earl of Oxford to take him to the Tower 'to preserve him from doing hurt either to the king's service or to himself'.[22] Henry supposedly remarked that 'if he were hys frende . . . he should not be miscontented to suffre so lytle a reproche & rebuke for his princes pleasure',[23] and he remained in custody until the danger was past.

Dorset commanded no army of retainers and was never regarded as the leader of a faction, so why did Henry think him too dangerous to be left at liberty? The most likely reason is that he possessed information that could prove highly embarrassing if he chose to reveal it, and he had perhaps threatened to do so (or was suspected of trying to make contact with Richard), when the King, rather mysteriously, offered to pardon and admit him to favour in June 1492. This was no ordinary pardon, however. Dorset had to agree to surrender all his manors save two to a group of trustees with the assurance that if, and only if, he remained loyal to Henry the arrangement would become void on his death and his heir would be allowed to inherit according to law. He also had to grant the King his son's wardship and marriage, give a personal recognizance of £1,000, and find sureties who would agree to forfeit £10,000 if he reneged on any part of his undertaking. The Earl of Kent, Viscount Lisle, Lord Grey of Codnor, Lord Grey of Wilton and fifty-one others bound themselves in a total of £9,225 for him, and Lord de la Warre was persuaded to pledge an additional £500 to guarantee his loyalty during his lifetime in February 1495. The arrangement was ended some time before August 1499 (two years before Dorset's death), but it had threatened him with almost total ruin while it lasted. Professor Lander comments that 'if the king's treatment of the Earl of Northumberland is considered humiliating' (Northumberland had been obliged temporarily to cede some of his estates to the Crown also), 'there are hardly words left to describe his dealings with Thomas Grey'.[24]

It could be argued that all or much of this is connected with Dorset's attempt to desert Henry in France before Bosworth, but, again, it made no sense to restrain or punish him so long afterwards unless the danger he posed was still current. The King never said why he chose to treat him so harshly, and in the absence of any obvious reason we can only assume that they both knew *something*, a dangerous secret that Henry was determined should always remain hidden. A recent biographer has called the Marquess 'a man of mediocre abilities who owed his place in English politics to his mother's unexpected marriage with Edward IV',[25] and it is a reasonable assumption that Henry would have paid little attention to him in other circumstances. He remained loyal, even helping to suppress the Cornish rebels in 1497, and became one of the few close male relatives of Elizabeth Woodville to die in his bed.[26]

This might have been the end of the matter, but Dorset's son, Thomas, the second marquess, who must have known the reason for his father's ill-treatment, seems to have been yet another thorn in Henry's side. The *Chronicle of Calais* recorded that

Ser Richard Carow knight, lievetenaunt of the castle of Caleys, browght owt of England, by the kyng's comaundement, the lord marques Dorset and the lord William of Devonshire the erle of Devonshire's sone and heyre [William Courtenay Catherine of York's husband], whiche were bothe of kynne to the late qwene Elizabethe and of hir blode. They had bene in the towre of London a greate season. They were kepte prisoners in the castle of Caleys as longe as kynge Henry the Seventhe lyved, and shulde have bene put to deathe, yf he had lyved longar. They were browght in to the castle of Caleys the xviij. of Octobar the xxiij. [year] of Henry the Seventhe [1508].[27]

Courtenay had offended Henry by colluding with the Earl of Suffolk (see below) and had been in prison since 1503, but there is no record of what Dorset had done – or was alleged to have done – nor was he ever brought to trial. He was kept in prison for a long time and there were real fears that the suspicious old King was about to silence him, but either he lacked evidence or the real reason could not be stated in open court. We know from other accounts that there was then no assumption that Prince Henry would automatically succeed his father, and the King undoubtedly feared for the future of his dynasty. Sir Hugh Conway remembered how, when Henry was ill on a previous occasion, he was amongst

many grett personages, the whiche fele in communicacion of the kyngis grace and of the world that shouldbe after hym yf hys grace hapned to depart. Then he said that some of them spake of my lorde of Buckyngham [Edward Stafford, son of the duke executed by Richard III], sayng that he was a noble man and woldbe a ryall ruler. Other ther were that spake, he said, in lykwyse of your troytor [traitor] Edmond De la Pole [Suffolk], but none of them, he said, spake of my lord prynce [Arthur or Henry].[28]

Dorset may have been one of the lords who Conway heard thinking aloud and he may have expressed similar views on other occasions; but was his preferred candidate Buckingham or de la Pole or Prince Richard, of whom Conway knew nothing? The King did not arrest Buckingham and only seized de la Pole when he challenged him openly – the impression is again that it was not so much what Dorset said that mattered but what he knew.

We will probably never know precisely what it was that the first and second Marquesses of Dorset had done to rouse the King's anger against them, but his difficulties with three of the sons of the Duke of Suffolk and his wife Elizabeth Plantagenet (the Yorkist kings' sister) were more transparent. The eldest,

John, Earl of Lincoln, had been Richard III's heir presumptive until Henry Tudor slew his uncle and seized the Crown at the battle of Bosworth. He appears to have accepted the change of government even when his great offices, his lieutenancy of Ireland and his headship of the King's northern household and council, were taken from him and given to others; but he was inevitably courted by Yorkist dissidents, who sensed his disappointment at the turn of events. He may have considered joining Lovel's northern uprising in 1486, but it was not until early in 1487 that he openly threw in his lot with the Simnel rebels and crossed to Burgundy. He was killed leading the Yorkist army at the battle of Stoke on 16 June, notwithstanding that Henry had ordered that he was to be taken alive if at all possible because 'he suspected that there must be yet further members of the conspiracy who, at a convenient time and place, would join with the rebels'.[29] Lord Bacon says that the Earl and his friends had agreed that the impostor Simnel would be 'put down' if the insurrection succeeded and the '*true Plantagenet received*' (emphasis added).[30] Readers have assumed that his curiously worded phrase referred to young Warwick (on whose behalf the rebellion had been organised), but it could also have applied to Prince Richard. Lincoln may well have based 'his particular hopes' on the 'true Plantagenet' gaining the kingdom, but that is not to say that he hoped to become king himself.

The Duke of Suffolk played no part in his son's treasons, and Edmund, his next heir (born *c.* 1472), was fortunately too young to be implicated. He was still technically a minor when his father died in 1492, and the loss of the family manors forfeited by Lincoln meant that he lacked the means to maintain ducal status. A compromise was agreed by which he accepted the reduced title of Earl of Suffolk in return for being allowed to enter some of his brother's former properties, but he also had to pay the Crown £5,000 in yearly instalments of

£200 during the lifetime of his mother and £400 per annum after her death. He was created a Knight of the Garter in 1495 and helped defeat the Cornish rebels at Blackheath in June 1497; but the harsh terms of the settlement probably rankled, and he may have felt humiliated when the King required him openly to 'plead his pardon' (Bacon), after he was accused of murdering one Thomas Crue in 1499. This may have prompted his first flight abroad (an excursion from which he was soon persuaded to return and again submit to Henry), but more difficulties followed, and he again left England without permission in August 1501. This time Henry was less lenient. Sir James Tyrell, who, interestingly, had shown himself favourably disposed towards Edmund was executed, and William Courtenay and other friends were imprisoned. He remained abroad for five years, short of money and tolerated, rather than actively assisted, by the European powers, until finally, in 1506, he again surrendered to Henry in return for an assurance that he would not be harmed personally. The King kept his part of the bargain, but Yorkist intrigues continued, and he was executed by Henry VIII in 1513.[31]

It is usually assumed that Suffolk, like Lincoln, wanted to be king, but he never, so far as is known, made any statement to this effect or styled himself 'Edmund I'. This may imply that his aim was to crown Prince Richard (recovering his lands and dukedom in the process), and there is perhaps some hint of this in a letter that Richard (his younger brother who had shared his second exile) wrote to him in 1505. Richard, who had been left at Aachen as security for Edmund's debts there, began by 'ombully' recommending himself and continued: 'Sir, I beseche your grace gyf credens to Stase [the bearer, Eustace] towchyng soche mater as ys brokyn to me of, and of the said matyr that I may shortly have answare how ye wyll stonde in thys cawse.'[32] There is, of course, no proof that the 'mater' concerned the lost prince, but there were clearly secrets that the brothers dared not commit to writing in case their correspondence fell into the wrong hands.

Richard remained on the Continent when Edmund returned to England and evaded Henry's attempts to capture him by commending himself to King Ladislas of Hungary, who had married his cousin. He subsequently fought for Kings Louis XII and Francis I of France against various enemies (including England), and was killed on the French side at the battle of Pavia in Lombardy in 1525. Schemes to invade England via Scotland and Ireland had come to nothing, and the saga of the de la Poles, opposition to the first Tudors – which had spanned almost four decades – ended with his death.[33] He had been recognised by Louis XII as the rightful king of England in 1512, but as three of his elder brothers, Edmund, Humphrey and William, were still then living, it may be assumed that the French king was merely serving his own ends.

There can be little doubt that many of the European rulers who supported Edmund and Richard from time to time used them – or hoped to use them – for their own political purposes, but they lost a genuine friend when their aunt Margaret, Duchess of Burgundy, died in November 1503. Margaret was always Henry's most implacable opponent – Vergil says that she pursued him 'with insatiable hatred and with fiery wrath'[34] – and the failure of the Simnel rebellion had not deterred her from helping Perkin Warbeck in the 1490s. She affected to believe that Warbeck really was her nephew, but Perkin seems to have been less certain. He told his interrogators after he was captured that he was only a substitute or stand-in,[35] but a substitute for whom? The unfortunate Warwick was still a possibility, but it is surely more likely that he was a substitute for the person whose identity he had borrowed – Prince Richard of York. He had doubtless enjoyed his years of being fêted in the courts of Europe, and would have been well provided for in the new world he had helped to make.

King Henry was unlikely to be troubled by men such as
Oliver King and Andrew Dymock – they had been promoted
and were hardly of the stuff of kingmakers – but his dealings
with Piers Curteys, who had supplied clothes to the young
Prince Richard, seem to have been rather less easy. Curteys was
restored to his former offices in September 1486 'in
consideration of his true heart and service and of the great
persecution, dangers and losses of goods, sustained by him in
the king's cause, he having kept sanctuary at Westminster long
time in sadness, punishment and fear, awaiting the king's
arrival'.[36] He was one of those who had loyally served Edward
IV but had been unable to accommodate himself to King
Richard, just the kind of man Henry needed; but he still found
it prudent to sue for pardons in March 1492 and February
1495. He may have wavered when the Warbeck conspirators
tried to draw him into their schemes by playing on his previous
loyalty to Prince Richard, but he would surely have lost his
offices if the authorities thought he had seriously encouraged
them. A change of government – and the restoration of Edward
IV's son to his 'right' – would not, perhaps, have been
unwelcome to him, but the potential benefits of a successful
uprising had to be weighed against the risks.[37]

The rebels may have met with a number of refusals as they
cast about for support in England, but one – perhaps rather
surprising – individual who was persuaded to abet treason was
William Worsley, the Dean of St Paul's. Worsley was an able
and intelligent administrator whose rise in the Church had been
assisted by his kinsmen, William and Laurence Booth, who had
both become archbishops of York. He successfully transferred
his allegiance from Edward IV to Richard III and then to Henry
VII (he apparently saw no reason to seek a pardon from Henry
for having served Richard), and by 1494 was almost 60 and
had been Dean of St Paul's for some sixteen years. He was one
of four senior clergymen arrested at the beginning of 1495 for

his alleged involvement with the Pretender, but spent only sixteen weeks in the Tower before being pardoned. This could imply that he had been on the fringes of the conspiracy rather than a prime mover, but he was still deprived of his archdeaconry of Taunton, obliged to grant an annual rent of £200 to several named courtiers, and had to find eight mainpernors who each pledged £200 for his future loyalty. It was a rather disappointing end to an otherwise rewarding career.[38]

Writers have speculated that Worsley joined the conspiracy because Henry VII had not appointed him to a bishopric, but would an old man who already enjoyed a secure and privileged existence have risked everything for a few short years as a member of the episcopacy? It could be argued that the plotters had tricked him into believing that Warbeck was genuine, but it is more probable that it was his knowledge of the real prince that persuaded him to change the habit of a lifetime. The majority of his estates lay in, or close to the borders of, Essex, and a group of manors in the north-east of the county, Ardleigh, Walton le Soken, Thorpe le Soken and Kirby le Soken, were within easy distance of Colchester. He almost certainly knew Abbot Stansted well enough to call on him at St John's on the occasions when he was in the area, and Stansted may well have been tempted quietly to show him a young man who, although now a bricklayer, had once been a prince. This would have transformed what, until then, had seemed to be just another imposture that might – or might not – change the world for the better, and, unlike Curteys, he had the courage of his convictions. The conspiracy became the means of attaining an entirely justifiable end.

There is, of course, no absolute proof that the actions and attitudes of these various men and women were conditioned by the knowledge that Prince Richard was still living, and it could be argued that those who promoted the claims of the young

Earl of Warwick thought that no better candidate was available to them. But was Warwick – who was debarred by his father's attainder, perhaps simple minded, and wholly inexperienced in government – ever meant to be more than a stalking horse, a substitute for the real claimant whose life they dared not endanger, and did they consider him expendable if they failed and the worst came to the worst? Warwick, locked in the Tower, could do nothing wrong himself; but in 1499 Henry allowed him to fraternise with the then captive Warbeck and executed both of them for planning to escape! It was Ferdinand and Isabella who had insisted that the King destroy his rival before they would allow their daughter Catherine to marry Prince Arthur; but they would have known nothing of Richard at distant Colchester (at least not for the moment), and Henry was not about to tell them! Warwick died because he was the obvious, visible, Yorkist claimant: the secret one lived on.

# EIGHT

## *'Cousin' Henry*

Henry VII died on 21 April 1509, rich, austere and respected rather than loved by his subjects. The uncertainties of the earlier years of his reign were fast becoming memories, and no one doubted any longer that Henry, Duke of York, his eldest surviving son, would succeed him. Queen Elizabeth of York had gone to her grave in 1503, a year after the sudden death of the royal couple's eldest son Prince Arthur; but none of these events made any perceptible difference to a man working as a bricklayer at Colchester (and perhaps at other sites in East Anglia), who was now approaching middle age. The time between Henry VIII's accession and the dissolution of St John's Abbey and the other English monasteries occupies a period of almost thirty years in Richard's life, but they were years in which the threat he posed to the new dynasty perceptibly diminished and the government accordingly took less interest in him. It is unlikely that many Englishmen would have shifted to replace Henry VIII with a now elderly and unknown son of Edward IV by 1539 (and perhaps considerably before then), even if they had learned that one still existed. King Henry destroyed a number of potential

'Yorkist' claimants, but Richard's anonymity preserved his life throughout the second Tudor king's reign much as it had in the years before 1509.

The new king confirmed and amplified the general pardon that his dying father had extended to all his subjects, but forgiveness was denied to the Earl of Suffolk and some others who were deemed dangerous or whose crimes were too serious to be forgotten. Richard was not mentioned, of course – he had done nothing wrong and did not even officially exist – but he may have felt less than comfortable now that a young ruler who was entirely unknown to him had taken over. He may, therefore, have sought to protect himself, and the first volume of the monumental *Letters and Papers, Foreign and Domestic, of the Reign of Henry VIII*, contains a pardon granted to 'Richard Grey of Colchester, alias of North Creke, Norf., yeoman or labourer' at Greenwich on 31 January 1512. The patent roll amplifies this to 'Richard Grey, late of Colchester, Essex, yeoman, alias Richard Grey of North Creke, Norf., yeoman, alias Richard Grey of Creke, Norf., Labourer, alias Richard Grey of North Creke, Norf., labourer',[1] but does not, unfortunately, record any other personal details or describe his offence. Was this 'our' Richard, and what can we glean from the entry if it was?

'Richard Grey' was not an uncommon name in the later fifteenth century – it was even the name of one of Richard's two half-brothers – and perhaps he had chosen, or been given, it for precisely this reason. He could not have called himself 'Richard Plantagenet', of course, and both Richard Fitzroy and Richard of Shrewsbury would have drawn unwelcome attention to him. Richard III had referred to his mother as 'Dame Elizabeth Grey' in the Act of Parliament that declared his parents' marriage invalid, and this would have been her name when Richard was born in 1473 if she had always been Edward IV's mistress and not his queen. King Edward's bastard son Arthur 'Plantagenet' had been known as Arthur Wayte (his mother's maiden name) in his earlier years, and so 'Grey' would have seemed entirely appropriate for Richard in the circumstances.[2] The terms 'yeoman' and 'labourer' could imply that he was known in the locality as a skilled if unpretentious craftsman,[3] and the appellation 'alias of North Creke, Norfolk' would suggest that he had been allowed to work away from St John's and Colchester (perhaps for a considerable period), when the abbot had little or nothing for him to do.

Creake Abbey, situated on the southern edge of the Burnhams and close to Walsingham, was a small house of Augustinian canons founded as a chapel and hospital by Sir Robert and Lady Alice de Nerford in the early years of the thirteenth century. Lady Alice gave the property to the Crown after she was widowed, and, when fire severely damaged the church and conventual buildings two and a half centuries later, the abbot and canons asked Richard III, their then patron, to help them rebuild. Richard, 'moved with pite' and concerned that 'by occasione wherof the said monasterie is like to falle to extreme desolacion and devine service to be withdrawene and diminisshed',[4] gave them £46 13s 4d from the revenues of the Duchy of Lancaster manor of Fakenham (Norfolk), and work commenced shortly after 20 February 1484. It was still in progress when Sir William Calthorpe of North Creake left £74 6s in his will dated 31 May 1494 (proved 27 November following) for the repair of the choir and presbytery and 'yf eny remayne' the 'chapell wythin ye same place wher ye annceterys of me ye said Sir William lye buryed';[5] and when Walter Aslak, lord of the manor of Bardolf in Great Ringstead, willed all his lands in Holme and Great Ringstead to the abbey so that 'the Ile on the north-syd of the queer [choir] in the seyd abbey be made wyth Tymber wormanshype' in February 1503/4.[6] But the monks had decided from the outset not to rebuild the nave and transepts (evidence, perhaps, of declining numbers as well as of a lack of resources), and when Giles Sheryngton, or Skevington, the last abbot, died on 12 December 1506, there was no one to succeed him and the property escheated to the Crown.

Writers have speculated that the canons of Creake had been wiped out by plague or another epidemic, but there may never have been more than six or seven of them even in the fourteenth century.[7] It is clear that craftsmen from elsewhere would have been needed to help restore the abbey, and Richard the bricklayer may have been 'loaned' or seconded for a period of years. He may have journeyed from Colchester to Creake in the mid-1490s (when he would have been in his early twenties), and remained there until work finally ended either shortly before, or shortly after, Abbot Sheryngton's death. Henry VII gave the abbey, together with its extensive holdings in Norfolk, Leicestershire and Northamptonshire, to his mother, Lady Margaret, in 1507, and she used it to endow Christ's College, her new foundation at Cambridge. The Master and Fellows of Christ's repaired the ruins (which had subsequently been used for farming purposes), in 1864, and sold the site of the church and the cloistral buildings into private ownership in 1930. The church was placed in the care of the then Ministry of Public Building and Works in 1950, and it is thanks to their efforts that this quiet out-of-the-way corner of north-east Norfolk can be visited with such pleasure today.

Richard doubtless worked at other locations for a period of months or even years as the sixteenth century lengthened, but these excursions have left no trace in the record. It is likely that the restrictions placed on him were progressively lifted as time passed, and that he came to enjoy as much freedom as the other lay brethren whose labour allowed the monks of St John's to live as gentlemen. He would have been required to attend some services of course (sitting in the nave of the abbey church screened from the religious in the choir), but his work was interesting, his place comfortable and his food plentiful. It was a far cry from life in a palace, but there was a comradeship, a sense of belonging, which compared favourably with the exclusiveness of his days as a prince.

Readers may wonder why Richard was trained as a bricklayer instead of being given a more educated, or 'white-collar' role in the establishment. The answer may be partly that the latter would have allowed him to retain his princely manner and bearing (something the authorities would have regarded as entirely inappropriate if their purpose was to bury his royal persona), but also because working with bricks was a speciality of the East Anglian region. The art of creating patterns with blue bricks on a red background had been introduced into the eastern counties by Flemings in the fifteenth century, and in Richard's time would have been regarded as a 'growth' industry, something a young man could usefully learn in the knowledge that there would always be a demand for his services.[8] He would soon have realised, or been made to realise, that he must adapt to his new role if he wanted to help both himself and others, and only a trace of gentility – his liking for reading – remained in the end.

Abbot Stansted, Richard's protector and guardian, died in 1497 and was succeeded by William Lyndesey (or Sprowton), who lived until 1517. Abbot John Stoke, who resigned in 1523, was followed by Abbot Thomas Barton (1523–33), and lastly by Abbot Thomas Marshall (or Beche), who presided over St John's until the dissolution of 1539. All these men must have known the true identity of their lay brother, but Richard caused no trouble and so no one troubled him or them. The daily round of life at the abbey had already existed for four centuries and seemed likely to continue indefinitely; but there were still incidents or moments of excitement that offered a single and occasionally bored young man some momentary distraction. Relations between the monks and the townsmen of Colchester were often difficult, and there were frequent disputes between them concerning alleged trespass and rights over land. A note added to the abbey's leger book tells how

in the V[th] yere of Kyng Herry the VII[th] [1490], the communys [commons] of the towne of Colchester brak the fense and closure of Marylands [part of the abbey's estate], and put in their catell claymyng the seyd lands as theyre commune [common pasture]. And thereuppon Dawn [Dom] William Bury, that tyme beyng celerer of the monastery of Seynt Johns, the viij[th] day of Septembre in the seyd yere of Kyng Herry the VII[th] distreyned the catall of Roberd Lawson, glasyer, John Austyn, lymebrenner [lime-burner], and Thomas Gybbeson there fowndyn, and draffe [drove] ther catall to the pownde of the seyd monastery, and so kept the seyd catall till the seyd Roberd Lawson and Thomas Gybbeson cam till [to] th' abbot of the seyd monastery and yaffe [gave] him viijd. that is to say every [each] of them iiijd. for trespas . . . with ther catall done. And the seyd John Austyn yaffe [gave] *di' quart'* [half a quarter of] lyme to the seyd abbot for trespas there with hys catall done.

The abbot was a powerful landlord, and there can be little doubt that the townsmen regarded him and his more aggressive acolytes with a fair measure of dislike and caution. We read that

Dawn [Dom] William Miche in the ix[th] day of Octobyr in the seyd yere distreyned the catall of John Flyngaunt and in lyke wyse draffe [drove] it to the seyd pownde. And than cam a chylde of the seyd John's pryvely [secretly] and set [let] the catall ought [out] of the seyd pownde unknowyng at that tyme to the seyd abbott's officerys. But whan it was aspyed [noticed] that the seyd chylde had so done the seyd John

The south prospect of St John's Abbey church, Colchester (from Philip Morant, *The History and Antiquities of the Most Ancient Town and Borough of Colchester* (1748), facing p. 36).

Flyngaunt browghte the seyd cattal ayene [again] to the seyd pownde and desyred that he myghte have his cattall delyvered, and because he browghte it ayene so curteysely he had hys catall delyvered and payd but 1d. for hys trespas in the seyd lands done with hys catall. Also the seyd Dawn William Miche dystreyned the horsys of Roberd Rookwood gentilman, Roberd Kene, son of the seriowntis [serjeant] of the said towne and —— Cowper in the secunde day of Septembyr in the viij[th] yere of the seyd Kyng, and draffe them to the seyd pownde. Whych Roberd Rookwood, Roberd Kene, and —— Cowper cam to the seyd Abbot and agreyd with the seyd Abbot for trespas so there done with ther seyd horse [their horses were returned to them].

Also the seyd Dawn William Miche dystreyned the horse of Thomas Ball in the xx[th] of Septyembyr in the ix[th] yere of the seyd Kyng and draffe yt to the seyd pownde, whych Thomas Ball cam to the seyd Abbot and agreyd with the Abbot for the trespas so there done with hys horse.[9]

The impounding of animals whose owners found themselves on the wrong side of Abbot Stansted was clearly a regular feature of life in Colchester, and gentlemen and officials of the town were spared no more than peasant farmers. One wonders if the 'chylde' of John Flyngaunt who released his cattle was acting on his own initiative, or whether his father had contrived the situation to 'prove' his own goodwill and honesty and so escape with a smaller penalty? If so, he succeeded very well.

Another brief moment of curiosity, excitement even, occurred many years later in 1535. Richard Jonson and his wife of Bucsted by Colchester wrote, presumably to Thomas Cromwell:

'Ombly compleyning unto yowr gudnes your poor bed[beads]man' . . . that about Shrovetide was twelvemonth [since] they were brought to Fullam, imprisoned by the bishop of London till harvest, and compelled to abstain from flesh till Whitsuntide, besides being so scantily fed that they would sooner have died. Nothing could be proved against them, and the Bishop was commanded by the King to deliver them and others whom he had in prison, but he conveyed them to Colchester, and imprisoned them in the abbey of St John's worse than before. Those who of their charity ministered to them were 'so opprobriously said to that they durst come no more at us', and they continued in misery till Michaelmas when they escaped. Have kept close ever since, and dare not be seen openly for fear of the Bishop.[10]

There is no indication of how the Jonsons had offended the bishop, nor do we know why he chose to send them to St John's rather than release them. Their complaint may have been

1. Richard, Duke of York. Detail from 'royal' window, Canterbury Cathedral, *c.* 1482.

2. Edward, Prince of Wales (Edward V). Figure from fifteenth-century glass installed by Bishop Alcock, Little Malvern Priory, Worcestershire.

3. Edward IV. Panel portrait.

4. Elizabeth Woodville. Panel portrait with the added inscribed date '1464', the year of her marriage to Edward IV (ex coll. W.A. Shaw, present location unknown).

5. Richard III. Panel portrait.

6. Henry VII and Elizabeth of York. Gilt bronze tomb effigies by Pietro Torrigiano, Westminster Abbey.

7. Henry VIII. Copy after the standard Holbein image.

8. 'The marriage of Richard of Shrewsbury, Duke of York, to the Lady Anne Mowbray', engraving after the painting by James Northcote, RA (1820).

9. Creake Abbey. The church from the west.

10. Creake Abbey. The south chapel from the crossing.

11. St Mary's Church, Eastwell. The tower, west wall, and south-west chapel from the north-east.

12. 'Richard Plantagenet's tomb' at Eastwell.

13. Modern plaque affixed to the tomb.

exaggerated – they survived for a long time on what were supposedly starvation rations – and their confinement at Colchester cannot have been too stringent, since friends were able to visit them and they eventually escaped. Richard would have been aware of these events, and it would be tempting to suppose that he was one of those who took pity on them; but the end of the story, like its beginning, is entirely unknown.

We do not know if Richard ever feared for his life during the long years of Henry VIII's reign, but he may have felt some apprehension if he learned of the fates of others whom the King thought might threaten his security. Henry VII had preferred bonds to violence (only once, in the case of the Earl of Warwick, was he moved to slay the innocent), but his son was altogether more ruthless. His reign is littered with the corpses of those he thought his enemies – from the Earl of Suffolk, executed in 1513, to the Earl of Surrey killed in 1547[11] – and Richard must have wondered if, at some time, he would himself fall victim to royal suspicion. Some of these executions were justifiable in that the victims had been either actively disloyal or at least blatantly incautious; but there could be no excuse for the butchering of the elderly Margaret Pole, Countess of Salisbury (George, Duke of Clarence's daughter), in 1541. Margaret's eldest son, Henry, Lord Montague, was executed in 1538 together with Henry Courtenay, Marquess of Exeter, and Sir Edward Neville, whose Yorkist blood also offended Henry; and she herself was sent to the block largely, it may be supposed, as a substitute for her second son, Reginald, Cardinal Pole, who was beyond the King's reach.

Margaret Pole was born at Farleigh Castle in Wiltshire on 14 August 1473, only three days before Prince Richard was born at Shrewsbury.[12] They were first cousins, and were brought up together at Sheen palace after her father's execution in February 1478. In 1491 she was married to Sir Richard Pole, the son of Lady Margaret Beaufort's half-sister (no connection of the de la Poles), and Henry VIII subsequently created her Countess of Salisbury in her own right. She was made governess to the infant Princess Mary, and stood high in royal favour until her son Reginald's opposition to the King's religious policies led to her dismissal and cast a shadow over the whole family. She was perhaps the person closest to Richard after his mother and younger sisters, and, again, there is every likelihood that she knew what had become of him and took a discreet interest in his well-being. She was arrested and attainted in 1539, but then spent nearly two years in the Tower 'tormented by the severity of the weather and insufficient clothing' before being executed on 27 May 1541.

No one has managed to explain why the King found it necessary to destroy a 67-year-old grandmother, and the discovery of a conspiracy in Yorkshire (which she could not have influenced) does not seem a very plausible reason. Again, it would be tempting to suggest that she died for her knowledge rather than her actions, but Henry VIII was now behaving so irrationally that no logical motives can be imputed to him. Thomas Cromwell, the King's chief minister, was arrested on 10 June 1540 (less than two months after being created Earl of Essex), and sent to his death for reasons that are as obscure as they are uncertain. He was brought low by enemies who resented his great authority, but we do not know how they managed to persuade Henry that he was guilty of high treason. The King described him as 'the most faithful servant he had ever had' only eight months later and accused some of traducing him on 'light pretexts';[13] but, if Cromwell went to his death somewhat bewildered, he was not alone. Two days after he was executed three reformist clergymen, including his close associate Robert Barnes and William Jerome, his vicar at Stepney, were burned at Smithfield as heretics, although it is unclear what they had done, or said, to deserve such a terrible sentence. Like Lady Margaret and Cromwell, they were convicted by act of attainder (which effectively prevented the flimsy nature of the charges against them from being challenged in open court), and, when Barnes asked the attending sheriff if he had 'any articles against me for the which I am condemned' and appealed to anyone in the crowd to tell him, if they could, 'wherefore I die, or that by my preaching hath taken error', the response he received was entirely negative. He and his friends were clearly baffled and bemused by what was happening to them, and even the chronicler Edward Hall, no mean admirer of the Tudors, confessed that he had never been able to understand why they were executed, 'although I have searched to know the truth'.[14] They were simply victims of a system that allowed men (and women) to be sent to their deaths because they had offended someone in the Henrician hierarchy (Barnes had earlier made a personal attack on Stephen Gairdner), and that *someone* had managed to persuade the fickle king, however momentarily, that they were a threat to his policies and the quiet of the realm.

Prince Richard was plainly at some risk in this situation, but may have drawn comfort – at least in earlier years – from the burgeoning career of his illegitimate half-brother Arthur Wayte (or Plantagenet[15]), whom we mentioned briefly above. Arthur was born, in all probability, a little before King Edward's marriage to Elizabeth Woodville (that is, *c.* 1462), and, like Richard, spent many of his formative years in obscurity. He was apparently always acknowledged and treated as a king's son – the royal tailor made various robes for him in 1472 – but there is no mention of him after 1483 until he was given a place in the household of his half-sister Elizabeth of York in 1501. After her death he transferred to the King's (Henry VII's) household, and became an esquire of the body to Henry VIII when Henry succeeded his father in 1509. We cannot explain how this mild-mannered, perhaps rather dull, man who was now approaching 50 became the trusted companion of the robust, confident, young monarch; but it was almost certainly Henry who arranged his first marriage to Elizabeth, daughter of Edward Grey, Viscount Lisle, in 1511. He succeeded to his father-in-law's title in 1523, was installed as a Knight of the Garter in 1524, was appointed vice-admiral of England the year following, and finally, became Lord Deputy, or governor, of Calais in 1533. Elizabeth had died in 1526, and three years later he married Honor Grenville, who was thirty years his junior but to whom he became very close. Their letters usually begin with 'my own sweetheart', and Honor concluded one of hers with the words 'her that is more yours than her own, which had much rather die with you there than live here'.

Arthur seems to have been well able to trim his sails to the prevailing political and religious climate, but his new wife was an unrepentant Romanist whose religious convictions sat ill with her husband's duty to defend Calais against Catholic France. It was also unfortunate that in 1538 he took into his household two men, Gregory Botolf and Clement Philpot, who, unbeknown to him, were determined to do what they could to reverse the religious revolution that had made Henry head of the English Church. Suspicion inevitably fell on Arthur and Honor when Botolf and Philpot's plot to deliver Calais to the French misfired two years later, and they were arrested and sent to the Tower on 19 May 1540. A search of their vast correspondence – some 3,000 letters spanning the seven years of Arthur's governorship – yielded no incriminating evidence, but they languished in prison for nearly two years, he 'in one small chamber, very narrow'. Eventually, he was permitted to take exercise on the walls, and it was there that he caught sight of the King as he was being rowed down the Thames from Westminster to Greenwich, and 'raised his hands high, and shouted hoarsely from the Tower where he was imprisoned for mercy and release from prison'. 'The king took it graciously' – perhaps even Henry would have been surprised if his doddering old uncle (whom he had once described as 'the gentlest heart living') had really been involved in a plot to betray him – 'and sent his secretary to the Tower to the lord to show him that the king had given him his pardon, and that he would have his freedom and release from prison two or three days later, and that he would get back his possessions and offices'. But when the secretary reached the Tower and brought Arthur the news, the old man became so excited that 'his heart was overcharged therewith' and he promptly collapsed and died! Honor, it is said, 'fell distraught of mind at the news and, according to Foxe, 'so continued many years after'. The moral of the story is that Arthur was safe while he was a nobody, but that, once he had achieved prominence, he was obliged to walk a tightrope to avoid falling foul of the King or Cromwell. He trod as warily as anyone could have, but even that was not enough.[16]

But we overrun ourselves. The terrible fate which overtook not only Margaret of Salisbury and her family but also Thomas Cromwell and his clerical associates (and which proved the undoing of Arthur Plantagenet) was inextricably bound up with King Henry's decision to divorce his first queen, Catherine of Aragon, in 1527. Only one of Catherine's many children – the Princess Mary – had survived infancy, and Henry chose to believe that, because he had offended God by marrying his late brother's widow contrary to the divine law of Leviticus, he was being punished by miscarriages, stillbirths, and, most importantly, the denial of a son. He badgered and battered the Pope, Clement VII, with a multiplicity of theological arguments, but Clement proved reluctant both to abrogate the dispensation granted by his predecessor, Julius II, and to risk offending the Emperor, Charles V, who was Catherine's nephew. The 'great matter' dragged on until Anne Boleyn, whom Henry intended to marry as soon as he was free to do so, became pregnant late in 1532. It was essential that the child be born in wedlock, and so Henry married Anne, probably in January, and had Thomas Cranmer, his Archbishop of Canterbury, annul his marriage to Catherine at Dunstable on 10 May. Pope Clement's response was to declare the first marriage valid, and his decision to impose sanctions on Henry for divorcing Catherine precipitated the break with Rome. Those who declined to recognise Henry as Supreme Head of the Church in England – Thomas More and John Fisher among them – paid the supreme penalty, and the great and the good began to walk a theological as well as a political tightrope as Henry considered how traditional or reformist his new church should be.

The King was himself theologically conservative and not unsympathetic to the traditionalist or Catholic faction led by the Duke of Norfolk; but Cromwell, Cranmer, and other 'evangelicals' with Protestant leanings were able to persuade him to publish the Bible in English and to undertake reform in two areas – by discouraging pilgrimages to shrines and by dissolving some lesser, impoverished monasteries whose closure would benefit the Crown financially. Wolsey had dissolved a number of smaller religious houses to finance his educational projects at Ipswich and Oxford, and it was now (1536) decreed that, unless specifically spared, all monasteries and nunneries with a gross income of less than £200 per annum would be taken into the King's hands. Some smaller, poorer houses were, in fact, allowed to continue, and all who wished to remain in the religious life were permitted to do so; but fears that the old ways were under attack, coupled with rumours that the government meant to strip parish churches and ban other elements of popular religion, fuelled the northern uprising known as the 'Pilgrimage of Grace'. The 'Pilgrimage' failed because – as in 1381 – the 'Pilgrims' trusted the word of a king who had no qualms about arresting and executing them once the heat had gone out of the situation; but it stung Henry into taking far more radical measures. Famous shrines such as the Holy Blood of Hailes in Gloucestershire, Our Lady of Walsingham in Norfolk, and St

Thomas of Canterbury were destroyed and their treasures carried away by the cartload (St Thomas, whose bones were burned, was denounced as a traitor), and the seizure of religious houses sympathetic to the Pilgrimage was followed by the dissolution of larger establishments which had not offended Henry and which Parliament had praised for their good moral standards in 1536. The King, who at least pretended to be even-handed, was as ready to execute the Catholic Poles as the allegedly heretical Cromwell; and any qualms of conscience were doubtless obviated by the vast windfall that now began to fall to the Crown.[17]

It was inevitable that the destroying hand of the royal commissioners would, in due course, fall upon St John's Abbey, and Dr Lee and William Cavendish were ordered to repair to and dissolve it on 6 November 1538. The abbot had secured the favour of Sir Thomas Audeley, the Chancellor, by exchanging lands and had paid the usual bribes to Cromwell; but the monks' cause had not been helped by John Francis, the sub-prior, who had been vociferous in his denunciation of the events of recent years. He had endorsed the comment made by another monk, John Flingant, that 'dispensations were hung up for sale in the apothecaries' shops in Rome with a blank for the buyer's name',[18] and said (among other things) that those who consented to the King's marriage to Anne Boleyn were heretics. These remarks were unlikely to endear them to Henry, but they both took the Oath of Supremacy on 7 July 1534 together with the abbot and fourteen other monks. St John's, which was valued at £523 16s 0¼d, was rich enough to escape the first, limited, dissolution, and, although Sir Thomas Audeley wrote to Cromwell on 8 September 1538 suggesting that it be converted to a secular college, he received no encouragement. His argument was that 'few of reputation would keep house there'[19] because it lacked water and that many poor people depended on it for relief; but neither the proffered royal right of presentation to the proposed new establishment, nor the offer of £1,000 for the King coupled with a £200 'backhander' for the minister, made any difference. These were fearful, uncertain days for those who lived in, or who relied upon, the abbey, including, we assume, a man now in his mid-sixties who for some fifty-five years had known no other life.

Sir Thomas Audeley may have been initially puzzled and disappointed when his suggestions were rejected, but the probability is that they were stymied by the behaviour of the last abbot of St John's, Thomas Marshall, or Beche. Marshall had had a number of conversations with individuals which he clearly intended should remain private, but which were reported to the government when it began to probe his alleged misdoings. He had allegedly said that 'the cause why the king forsook the bishop of Rome was to the intent that his majesty might be divorced from the Lady Dowager [Catherine of Aragon] and wed Queen Anne' (this was self-evident but entirely at odds with Henry's claim to have acted from the highest motives), and to have maintained that 'those who made the king supreme head were false heretics and cursed to God's own mouth'. One witness, his servant Edmund Trowman, had heard him express his support for the northern Pilgrims, and Thomas Nuthake, physician and mercer, reported that he had been highly critical of the executions of More and Fisher: 'Nuthake, alas, what wretched tyrants and bloodsuckers be these that have put to death and martyred these blessed clerks and best learned men that were in this realm. They died martyrs and saints, in my conscience, for holding with our holy father the pope for the right of all holy church.' He had also remarked that 'God will take vengeance at length for the putting down of these houses of religion', and claimed that 'two or three of the king's council had brought his grace to such a covetous mind that if all the water in [the] Thames did flow gold and silver it were not able to quench his grace's thirst'.[20]

The Seal of Colchester Abbey (from *The Victoria County History of Essex*, vol. 2, ed. W. Page and J. H. Round (1907)).

Marshall had expressed the conviction that 'the kyng shall never have my howse . . . for I knowe by my lernyng that he cannot take yt by right and lawe', but Sir John Seyncler, his confidant on this occasion, replied that he should 'beware of suche lerning, for if ye holde suche lernyng as ye lernyd at Oxenforde when ye were yonge ye wil be hanged'. He was in the Tower by 20 November 1539, and tried to excuse himself by claiming he had really hoped that the Pilgrims would be vanquished 'as the Cornysshemen were', and that, although he believed that More and Fisher 'wer grett lernyd men' (no one could have doubted this), he trusted they would be forgiven their sins. He fully accepted the royal supremacy (the pope, he now alleged, 'usurpid moch more autoryte than ever was gyve to hym by any law'), and denied saying that all the water in the Thames would not slake Henry's covetousness. 'I have sayde that the nature of coveytise is lyke to the dropsy, it is insaciable and never content, but I never referith the same saynge to the kyngges grace nor yet to his most honourable counsell.' Finally, he claimed he had resisted the dissolution of his house only to increase his pension, 'and yff it be the wyll of God so to be it is well doon'.[21]

None of these protestations availed him anything of course, and he was shortly afterwards sent back to Colchester to be tried by a commission headed by the Earl of Essex and five local knights, including his erstwhile friend Sir John Seyncler. He was hanged in the town on 1 December 1539, but it is unclear if he was also drawn and quartered (as were numbers of religious who had resisted Henry) or whether his retractions had at least served to make his ending more dignified. Sir Christopher Jenny, another of his judges, writing to Cromwell shortly afterwards, commented that 'the prisoner, after his judgement, axed [asked] the kyngs highness, yr lordeshippes and my lord chauncellors forgiveness and [ac]knowlegid hymself in substaunce to be giltie accordynge to theffect of the indictmente and shewyd hym self to be very penytent'. But he still, Jenny remarked, 'stoode somewhat in his own conceyte that the subpression of abbeys should not stonde with the lawes of God, and therby and by other circumstaunces I thought hym an evill man . . .'.[22]

These were dramatic days at Colchester, not least for those who had known Abbot Marshall as their spiritual father and as someone who had made all recent decisions affecting their lives for them. The monks of St John's were treated well enough: two brethren, John Fraunce and William Ryppner, received pensions of £6 13*s* 4*d* and £5 respectively (£5 per annum was an average, adequate payment), and they and others doubtless sought, and obtained, livings that added considerably to their incomes. Lay brothers who had worked on the land would have been needed by an estate's new owner or owners, but domestic servants probably lost their jobs, at least until there was a new family in residence.[23] Sir Thomas Audeley was denied the prize he had hoped for (though he held the abbey for a time 'at farm'), and it was leased to Sir Thomas Darcy for twenty-six years on 20 August 1546. Darcy subsequently sold the lease to one John Lucas, and it was probably only after this that craftsmen were required to redevelop the buildings; but there were others – men like Sir Thomas Wriothesley at Titchfield Abbey and Lord Sandys at Mottisfont Priory – who were anxious to move into their newly acquired properties as soon as possible. The services of bricklayers and others must have been much in demand in the wider world, and it is likely that Richard decided to leave Colchester when it became apparent that there would be no work for him there in the immediate future. This would have been no small upset for a man in his late sixties (very elderly by medieval and Renaissance standards), but he presumably found employment in the southeast that occupied him for a year or two until, finally, he came to Eastwell in 1542 or 1543. And the rest, as they say, is history.

# NINE

## *King Richard IV?*

Henry VIII died on 28 January 1547, never, in all probability, having met his uncle Richard or spared him a thought for many years. W.B. Nichols, in his novel *The Secret Son*, published in 1944, has the now elderly man being taken to London by a fearful Sir Thomas Moyle to meet the ruthless monarch who ruled his kingdom, but it is unlikely that Richard (or Moyle for that matter) ever considered placing his head in such an unpredictable lion's jaws. Richard may still have breathed a sigh of relief when he heard the news, since few with a claim to the throne could have thought themselves secure in the last pain-racked years of Henry's reign. Edward VI, his young son, was universally accepted as his father's successor, and would hardly have felt threatened by an obscure septuagenarian who had outlived all those who remembered his claim.

We said at the beginning that there can be no absolute certainty in these matters, and the Lost Prince is no exception. Many books have been written about King Arthur and Robin Hood (who may never have existed), and as many, if not more, have tried to probe the identity of the 'Man in the Iron Mask', identify who assassinated President Kennedy, or explain what happened on the *Mary Celeste*. None of them has so far succeeded, but that does not mean that every attempt to find a solution should be rejected because it falls short of a complete answer. Such works have extended the boundaries of our knowledge, and it is thanks to them that we now know a great deal more about these and other mysteries, even if we do not know as much as we would like. A long and deeply researched book like Ann Wroe's *Perkin* (another candidate for Richard of York) still leaves her subject's true identity open to question, but we would be much the poorer if it had not been written at all.

There are essentially two types of problems that confront anyone who delves into these mysteries. In the first, the answer may never have existed or may never have been known to any living person ('King Arthur' and the *Mary Celeste* are examples of this type), while in the second a number of individuals have been privy to the truth of the matter but have chosen not to reveal it. 'The Man in the Iron Mask' obviously falls into this category, but so too (in my opinion) does the fate of the Princes in the Tower and more particularly Prince Richard of York. Many commentators have assumed that the boys 'disappeared', and no one knew what had become of them; but no king or prince can be killed or kept in obscurity without someone giving the order and another (presumably) carrying it out. It might be possible to argue that the secret was known only to Richard III and died with him at Bosworth, but it is highly improbable that so many concerned relatives and former servants could have been fobbed off so easily. The inescapable conclusion is that some *did* know what had happened but preferred not to say.

The boys disappeared in Richard III's reign, and so it is usually assumed that he killed them, but this is by no means certain. Henry VII referred vaguely to the 'shedding of infants' blood' in the Act of Attainder passed against his slain rival and his supporters after Bosworth,[1] but Richard's supposed guilt was never used to justify Henry's success in overthrowing him. Henry, indeed, ignored the matter for seventeen years before publishing Sir James Tyrell's unlikely – and generally unaccepted – 'confession' in 1502, and apparently preferred to sweep it under the carpet rather than use it to make political capital. One possible explanation is that the Princes were killed by Henry Stafford, Duke of Buckingham, when he rebelled against King Richard late in 1483 and proposed making Henry king in his place. There can be little doubt that, if Buckingham did this, it was because he hoped to win the throne for himself, but Henry Tudor could not have avoided the aspersion that the Duke was acting on his behalf and with his approval. It would be quite understandable, therefore, if he did not wish the issue to be probed after his accession (a policy of 'least said, soonest mended' was clearly preferable to the tortuous process of trying to justify his innocence), but all this assumes that the boys had died and at the hands of Buckingham. There is, of course, no evidence that either of these things happened, and Henry would have been no less reluctant to discuss the matter if he knew that at least one them was still living. The new king's forthcoming marriage to their sister Elizabeth and his dependence on the Woodville faction meant that elimination was not an option;[2] and a number of senior figures were persuaded that it would be better for England if Prince Richard was to keep his life but lose his throne.

Henry's curiously negative response when Ferdinand and Isabella and others offered to help him 'prove' that Perkin Warbeck was an impostor – and his apparent failure to confront Warbeck with his 'sisters' – is also entirely explicable if he knew that Prince Richard was alive and well and living at Colchester. It is usually assumed that the King was either playing to the gallery or did not want to run the risk that

Perkin would be 'recognised' by one of Richard's relatives or former associates; but it is surely more likely that his polite rejection of all assistance mirrors a certainty that he could not, in reality, begin to justify. It would not have been unthinkable for Henry to execute his brother-in-law – Edward IV had, after all, sentenced his own brother to death – but it is most improbable that the reigning queen's brother would have been hung as a common criminal, as Warbeck was in 1499. There is no evidence that Queen Elizabeth turned against her husband – on the contrary, she continued to bear his children, and there is reason to think that their relationship deepened in the years prior to her death in 1503.[3] She does not seem to have minded that Warbeck's head was displayed on London Bridge or that his remains were interred in the Austin friars' church in Bread Street rather than with his 'ancestors' – but she had no need to if, as we suppose, she had long known of her brother's true fate.

Some of these points have been made above, but they are worth repeating if only to justify the premiss that compromise would have been essential if all the parties were to live and work together. Prince Richard could, theoretically, have been delivered from the obscurity to which Richard III had consigned him after the battle of Bosworth and could have claimed his rightful inheritance; but would Henry Tudor have surrendered the Crown he had recently risked everything to capture, and would others who had worked for the union of the two roses have wished to see the fruits of their labours snatched from them? How many would have been happy to see a 12-year-old child – even a son of Edward IV – replace the mature man upon whom so many hopes rested, and did anyone want to risk provoking a new war?

Our thesis, then, is that there is no evidence that the sons of Edward IV were killed by anyone. Edward V was very possibly ill and may have died within a short time of being deposed, whereupon his claim to the throne passed to his surviving younger brother. Buckingham's rebellion proved that declaring the boys illegitimate had failed to destroy their royal credentials, and Richard III decided that his remaining nephew must effectively 'disappear'. Killing the boy would have been the most awful betrayal of his late brother's trust, and so he was placed in the care of loyal followers who resided some distance from the capital. Richard's attitude towards him may have begun to change after his own son, Prince Edward, died in April 1484, and we cannot discount the possibility that the King intended to acknowledge him as his heir (a position that had remained officially vacant) after he had won the battle of Bosworth. But Richard's defeat and death meant that another plan had to be brought into action, and Francis Lovel took him to the safety and obscurity of St John's Abbey at Colchester, where remarkably, he was to spend many of the next fifty-five years.

Richard may have hoped that the marriage of the new king, Henry Tudor, to his sister Elizabeth would somehow lead to his own rehabilitation, but no king, and certainly not a new and insecure ruler like Henry, could tolerate a situation in which the man he had superseded was widely known in the country and about the court. Anonymity remained the only practical answer, and there seemed no reason why the arrangements that Richard III had made for him should not continue if Henry would benefit from them. He would have to be carefully monitored, of course (at least for the foreseeable future), and those who knew of his presence at Colchester warned that they must in no circumstances contact him or betray his identity to others; but, if this was done, there was no reason why he should not live out his life inconspicuously without troubling either Henry or later Tudor kings.

Most of those who knew of Prince Richard's survival were content to accept this situation, but Francis, Viscount Lovel, was clearly not. Lovel apparently assumed that his young charge would be safe at Colchester providing he did not use him as the figurehead of a new rebellion, and tried to make trouble for Henry from when he left St John's before Easter 1486 until his final defeat at the battle of Stoke fifteen months later. Henry hoped, indeed expected, that he would make his peace with the new government both during this period and in the aftermath of the Simnel rebellion, but no self-respecting king could allow a man who knew such a dangerous secret and rejected all attempts to conciliate him to remain in opposition and at liberty indefinitely. I have argued elsewhere that Henry left the door to a rapprochement open until it was apparent that Lovel was dead or no longer had information of value;[4] but he may not have done so if he had greater reason to fear him than has been supposed previously. The King may have decided, reluctantly, that, if Lovel would not submit, he must be eliminated; and so Tudor agents learned of his whereabouts and stabbed him as he sat in his chair in his secret hiding-place at Minster Lovel Hall. Such an idea may be rejected as preposterous (we do not even know for certain that the remains discovered at Minster Lovel in 1708 were Lovel's), but it is no more bizarre than some other theories advanced to explain his disappearance in the closing months of 1487 or the beginning of 1488.

This book has tried to show that Prince Richard *could* have survived the events of 1483 – at least on paper – but the potential stumbling block is the absence of anything that a modern court of law would accept as proof. The arrangement could work only if it remained a secret, carefully concealed from as many as possible, with little or nothing committed to writing. We cannot expect to find references to Prince Richard, even oblique ones, in official documents, and family members who engaged in 'loose talk' – whether verbally or in correspondence – would have been aware that they were placing his life in some danger. The only kind of 'evidence' that could – and did – survive is that which suggests that the government was unduly concerned with events at Colchester in the first half of Henry VII's reign. Lovel's 'unnecessary' journey, Henry's own visits, the secret mission undertaken by Philip Knighton and the strange restrictions imposed on Eleanor Kechyn can hardly be mere coincidences, but even these would fade from the picture as it became apparent that the plan had succeeded and Richard posed no threat to the Tudor monarchy. Cardinal Wolsey, Thomas More and Thomas Cromwell were almost certainly all aware of his existence, but by their day he had ceased to matter politically and could be left to live out his life in obscurity. By 1536 (the year of the Pilgrimage of Grace), few people of consequence would have remembered Edward IV personally, and those who did would have been in their sixties or seventies, too old to rise up on behalf of his son. Courtiers with Yorkist credentials went to the block because their very presence was evidence of their latent claims to the kingship; but Prince Richard was as out of sight as he was out of mind.

Richard's life was long, healthy and active and he may not have been dissatisfied with it, but the cataclysm that thrust him and so many others from the security of their monastic dwellings cannot be underestimated. By the late 1530s he was in his mid-sixties and doubtless looking forward to a peaceful retirement; but the dissolution of St John's made him effectively homeless and compelled him to travel to earn his bread. He carried his secret with him – as he had always done – until Sir Thomas Moyle caught him reading his Latin book and demanded to know how his bricklayer had acquired an education. Perhaps, just for a moment, Richard was moved to tell him everything, but some deep-seated instinct for self-preservation reasserted itself and he invented a story that admitted his royal origins but placed them firmly on the wrong side of the blanket. A bastard son of Richard III would have no claim on the throne (unlike the legitimate offspring of his elder

Plantaganet's (*sic*) cottage, Eastwell Church from the lake, and the artist's impression of Richard Plantagenet reading, drawn by X. Willis (from C. Igglesden, *A Saunter through Kent with Pen and Pencil*, vol. 3 (Ashford, 1901)).

brother), and yet could, at his father's discretion, have experienced much of the same privileged upbringing. He was aware that the curious Sir Thomas might try to probe further into his story, of course, and so made no mention of St John's or Colchester. The anonymity of London sufficed to cover his many 'hidden' years.

And what of the future? It is always possible that more documents will come to light, papers which may sound completely innocuous when read in isolation but which may take on added significance when viewed in the context of the above theory. The main hope of all those who are interested in the fate of the Princes is that the authorities will relent and allow a new examination of the bones preserved in Westminster Abbey, although, as we noted in Chapter One, it is far from certain that this would settle the matter to everyone's satisfaction. New evidence that they are the remains of Edward IV's sons would make it less likely that Richard of Eastwell and Prince Richard were one and the same person; but proof that they were not would at least leave the possibility open, and would (in the absence of any better explanation) make it more probable that the old man who died in 1550 was indeed one of the missing boys. The image of Prince Richard in the 'royal window' in Canterbury Cathedral still gazes down on visitors, as it has for the last five centuries;[5] while only a little over 12 miles away stand the crumbling ruins of Eastwell church and the remains of the tomb almost certainly erroneously associated with 'Richard Plantagenet'. Prince Richard . . . Richard Plantagenet . . . the names are identical and the geographical proximity seems almost more than coincidental. Did an elderly bricklayer ever pause to look into the face of his own portrait – a portrait from another life – on the occasions when he visited the greater church?

# APPENDIX ONE

## *Richard Plantagenet: A Legendary Tale*

The following was first published by Thomas Hull in 1774 with a dedicatory epistle to David Garrick, and is here reproduced from a photocopy in the Richard III Society Barton Library. The notes, which were designed to make the poem intelligible to a reader who knew nothing about Richard of Eastwell, have been omitted, as have the inverted commas at the beginning of each line and the numbers preceding the stanzas, but the original spelling, including the capitalisation, has been retained. It is long, but was written only fifty years after the Earl of Winchilsea first told Dr Brett the story, and is the work of no mean poet.

The following Poem fell into the Editor's Hands by a peculiar Means, which he is not at present permitted to reveal. He hopes the Singularity of the Story, and the moral Tendency, which so obviously and strongly inculcates THE DUTY OF A PATIENT SUBMISSION TO THE DESTINATIONS OF PROVIDENCE, IN ALL VICISSITUDES AND AFFLICTIONS OF LIEF, will justify his giving it to the World. He judged it too curious to be utterly lost; and his Desire to preserve it, induced him to collect, and scatter in Notes throughout the Work, such curious Particulars as (in his Judgment) prove the actual Existence of such a Person as RICHARD PLANTAGENET, and the chief Event of his Life to have been incontestibly certain.

Cover illustration from *Richard Plantagenet: A Legendary Tale*, by Mr Hull (1774).

THE Work is done, the Structure is compleat –
Long may this Produce of my humble Toil
Un-injur'd stand, and Echo long repeat,
Round the dear Walls, *Benevolence* and MOYLE!

So Richard spake, as he survey'd
The Dwelling he had rais'd;
And, in the Fullness of his Heart;
His gen'rous Patron prais'd.

Him MOYLE o'erheard, whose wand'ring Step,
Chance guided had that Way;
The Workman's Mien he ey'd intent,
Then earnest thus did say:

My Mind, I see, misgave me not,
My Doubtings now are clear,
Thou oughtest not, in poor Attire,
Have dwelt a Menial here.

To Drudgery, and servile Toil,
Thou couldst not be decreed
By Birth and Blood, but thereto wrought
By hard o'er-ruling Need.

Is it not so? That crimson Glow,
That flushes o'er thy Cheek,
And down-cast Eye, true Answer give,
And thy Tongue need not speak.

Oft have I mark'd thee, when unseen
Thou thought'st thyself by all,
What Time the Workman from his Talk
The Ev'ning Bell did call.

Hast thou not shunn'd thy untaught Mates,
And to some secret Nook,
With drooping Gait, and musing Eye,
Thy lonely Step betook?

There hath not thy Attention dwelt
Upon the letter'd Page,
Lost, as it seem'd to all beside,
Like some sequester'd Sage?

And wouldst thou not, with eager Haste,
The precious Volume hide,
If sudden some Intruder's Eye
Thy Musings hath descried?

Oft have I deem'd thou couldst explore
The Greek and Roman Page,
And oft have yearn'd to view the Theme,
That did thy Hours engage.

But Sorrow, greedy, grudging, coy,
Esteems of mighty Price
It's treasur'd Cares, and to the World
The scantiest Share denies;

All as the Miser's heaped Hoards,
To him alone confin'd,
They serve, at once, to soothe and pain
The wretched Owner's Mind.

Me had capricious Fortune doom'd
Thine Equal in Degree,
Long, long e're now, I had desir'd
To know thine History;

But who their worldly Honors wear
With Meekness chaste and due,
Decline to ask, lest the Request
Should bear Commandment's Hue.

But now thy Tongue hath spoke aloud
Thy grateful Piety,
No longer be thy Story kept
In painful Secrecy.

Give me to know thy Dawn of Life;
Unfold, with simple Truth,
Not to thy Master, but thy Friend,
The Promise of thy Youth.

Now, late in Life, 'tis Time, I ween,
To give thy Labours o'er;
Thy well-worn Implements lay by,
And drudge and toil no more.

Here shalt thou find a quiet Rest,
For all thy Days to come,
And every Comfort, that may serve
T'endear thy humble Home.

Hast thou a Wish, a Hope to frame,
Beyond this neat Abode?
Is there a Good, a higher Bliss,
By me may be bestow'd?

Is there within thine aged Breast
The smallest aching Void?
Give me to know thy Longings all,
And see them all supply'd

All I entreat, in Lieu, is this,
Unfold, with simple Truth,
Not to thy Master, but thy Friend,
The Promise of thy Youth.

So gen'rous MOYLE intent bespake
The long-enduring Man,
Who raised, at length, his drooping Head,
And, sighing, thus began.

RICHARD PLANTAGENET reciteth his TALE

HARD Talk to any, but thyself, to tell
The Story of my Birth and treach'rous Fate,
Or paint the Tumults in my Breast that swell,
At Recollection of my infant State!

Oft have I labour'd to forget my Birth,
And check'd Remembrance, when, in cruel wise,
From Time's Abyss she would the Tale draw forth,
And place my former self before my Eyes.

Yet I complain not, tho' I feel anew,
All as I speak, fell Fortune's bitter Spite,
Who once set Affluence, Grandeur, in my View,
Then churlish snatch'd them from my cheated Sight.

And yet it may be – is – nay, must be best,
Whate'er Heav'n's righteous Laws for Man ordain;
Weak Man! who lets one Sigh invade his Breast,
For earthly Grandeur, fugitive as vain!

Perchance Contentment had not been my Mate,
If in exalted Life my Feet had trod,
Or my Hands borne, in transitory State,
The Victor's Truncheon, or the Ruler's Rod.

My Curse, perchance, had been one dazzling Glare
Of splendid Pride, and I in vain had fought
The quiet Comforts of this humble Sphere,
Rest undisturb'd, and Reason's tranquil Thought.

But whither roam I? O! forgive, my kind,
My honour'd Lord, this undesign'd Delay,
Forgive, while in my new-awaken'd Mind
A Thousand vague Ideas fondly play.

Enough! – they're flown – and now my Tongue prepares,
Thou Source of every Good by me possest,
To pour a Tale into thy wond'ring Ears,
Full three-score Years close-lock'd within my Breast.

Of those Care-woven, long-protracted Years,
Some sixteen Summers pass'd obscurely on,
A Stranger to the World, its Hopes, and Fears,
My Name, Birth, Fortunes, to myself unknown.

Plac'd in a rural, soft, serene Retreat,
With a deep-learn'd Divine I held Abode,
Who fought, by pious Laws and Conduct meet,
The Way to Immortality and God.

By him instructed, I attain'd the sweet,
The precious Blessings that from Learning flow,
He fann'd in my young Breast the genial Heat,
That bids th' expanding Mind with Ardor glow.

He taught me with delighted Eye to trace
The comely Beauties of the *Mantuan* Page,
Enraptur'd mix with *Tully*'s polish'd Grace,
Or catch the Flame of *Homer*'s martial Rage.

Nor stopt he there, Preceptor excellent,
Nor deem'd that Wisdom lay in Books alone,
But would explain what moral Virtue meant,
And bid us make our Neighbour's Woes our own.

Heav'n's genuine Pity glist'ning in his Eyes,
The Sweets of Charity he would instill,
And teach what Blessedness of Comfort lies
In universal Mercy and Good-will.

So taught this pious Man, so thought, so did,
Squaring his Actions to his Tenets true;
His Counsel or Relief to none denied,
A gen'ral Good, like Heav'n's all-chearing Dew!

Thus guided, thus inform'd, thus Practice-drawn,
In guileless Peace my Spring of Life was spent,
My Leisure-hours I sported o'er the Lawn,
Nor knew what restless Care or Sorrow meant.

A courteous Stranger, ever and anon,
My kind Instructor's due Reward supplied;
But still my Name, my Birth, alike unknown,
Wrapt in the Gloom of Secrecy lay hid.

One Autumn-Morn (the Time I well recall)
That Stranger drew me from my soft Retreat,
And led my Footsteps to a lofty Hall,
Where State and Splendor seem'd to hold their Seat.

Thro' a long Range of spacious gilded Rooms,
Dubious I pass'd, admiring as I went,
On the rich-woven Labours of the Looms,
The sculptur'd Arch, or painted Roof intent.

My Guide, at length, withdrew; wrapt in suspense
And Fear I stood, yet knew not what I fear'd;
When straight to my appall'd, astounded Sense,
A Man of noble Port and Mein appear'd.

His Form commanded, and his Visage aw'd,
My Spirit sunk as he advanced nigh,
With stately Step along the Floor he trod,
Fix'd on my Face his penetrating Eye.

The dancing Plumage o'er his Front wav'd high,
Thick-studded Ribs of Gold adorn'd his Vest,
In splendid Folds his purple Robe did ply,
And royal Emblems glitter'd on his Breast

I sought to bend me, but my Limbs refus'd
Their wonted Office, motionless and chill;
Yet somewhat, as the Figure I perus'd,
A dubious Joy did in my Mind instill.

While thus I cow'r'd beneath his piercing Eye,
He saw and strove to mitigate my Fear,
Soft'ning the Frown of harsh Austerity
In his bold Brow, which Nature grafted there.

With Speeches kind he cheer'd my sinking Heart,
Question'd me much, and strok'd my drooping Head;
Yet his whole Mind he seem'd not to impart,
His Looks implied more than his Speeches said.

A broider'd Purse, which weighty seem'd with Gold,
He gave me then, and kindly press'd my Hand;
And thus awhile did stay me in his Hold,
And on my Face did meditating stand.

His Soul work'd hugely, and his Bosom swell'd,
As tho' some mighty Thing he yearn'd to say,
But (with indignant Pride the Thought repell'd)
He started, frown'd, and snatch'd himself away.

My Guide return'd, and reconducted me
Tow'rd the Abode of my Preceptor kind;
A Man he seem'd of Carriage mild and free,
To whom I thought I might unload my Mind.

Without Reserve I told him all that pass'd
Striving by mine his Confidence to gain;
Then my Enquiries frank before him cast,
Hoping some Knowledge of myself t'attain.

I ask'd what wond'rous Cause, yet undecsry'd,
Urg'd him his Time and Zeal for me t'employ;
And why that Man of Dignity and Pride
Had deign'd his Notice to a Stranger-Boy.

Confus'd, yet undispleas'd, my Guide appear'd,
Nought he divulg'd (tho' much he seem'd to know)
Save this, which he with earnest Look aver'd,
No Obligation, Youth, to me you owe;

I do but what my Place and Duty bid,
With me no Kindred-Drops of Blood you share,
Yet (hard to tell!) your Birth must still be hid;
Enquire no farther – Honour bids, forbear.

Thus he reprov'd, yet did it with a Look,
As tho' he pitied my Sensations keen;
Patient I bow'd me to his mild rebuke,
And pledg'd Obedience, with submissive Mein.

He left me at my Tutor's soft Abode,
And parting, bless'd me by the *holy Cross*;
My Heart wax'd-sad, as he re-trac'd the Road,
And seem'd to have sustain'd some mighty Loss.

But soon tumultuous Thoughts began give way,
Lull'd by the Voice of my Preceptor sage;
Unquiet Bosoms he could well allay,
His Looks could soften, and his Words assuage.

Unruly Care from him was far remov'd,
Grief's wildest Murmurs at his Breath would cease;
O! in his blameless Life how well he prov'd
The House of Goodness is the House of Peace!

Here I again enjoy'd my sweet Repose,
And taught my Heart, with pious Wisdom fill'd,
No more with anxious Throb to seek disclose
What stubborn Fate had doom'd to lie conceal'd.

But long these fond Delusions did not last,
Some sterner Pow'r my rising Life controul'd,
My visionary Hopes too swiftly past,
And left my Prospects dreary, dark, and cold.

When rugged *March* o'er-rules the growing Year,
Have we not seen the Morn, with treach'rous Ray,
Shine out awhile, then instant disappear,
Anf leave to Damp and Gloom the future Day?

So dawn'd my Fate, and so deceiv'd my Heart,
Nor wean'd me from my Hopes, but cruel tore;
In one unlook'd-for Moment, bade me part
From all my Comforts, to return no more.

My Guide once more arriv'd, tho'as of late,
Of soft Deportment he appear'd not now,
But wild Impatience flutter'd in his Gait,
And Care and Thought seem'd busy on his Brow.

'Rise Youth,' he said, 'and mount this rapid Steed' –
I argued not; his Bidding straight was done;
Proud-crested was the Beast, of warlike Breed,
Arm'd, at all Points, with rich Caparison.

We commun'd not – such Heat was in our Speed,
Scantly would it allow me Pow'r of Thought,
Till Eve deep-painted with a burning Red,
To *Bosworth Field* our panting Coursers brought.

Who hath not heard of *Bosworth*'s fatal Plain,
Where base Advent'rers did in Compact join
'Gainst Chiefs of Prowess high, and noble Strain,
And low'r'd the Crest of YORK's imperial Line?

Now verging on that memorable Ground,
Our Course we stay'd – yet we alighted not;
Fill'd with Astonishment I gaz'd around,
While in my glowing Breast my Heart grew hot.

Thick-station'd Tents, extended wide and far,
To th' utmost Stretch of Sight could I behold,
And Banners fluttering in the whistling Air,
And Archers trimly dight, and Prancers bold.

The sinking Sun, with richly-burnish'd Glow,
Now to his western Chamber made retire,
While pointed Spears, quick-shifting to and fro
Seem'd all as spiral Flames of hottest Fire.

Promiscuous Voices fill'd the floating Gale,
The Welkin echoed with the Steed's proud Neigh:
The Bands oft turn'd, and ey'd the Western Vale,
Watching the Closure of departing Day.

Light vanish'd now apace, and Twilight grey
With Speed unusual mantled all the Ground,
The Chieftains to their Tents had ta'en their Way,
And Centinels thick-posted watch'd around.

As sable Night advanced more and more,
The mingled Voices lessen'd by Degrees,
Sounding at length, as, round some craggy Shore,
Decreasing Murmurs of the ebbing Seas.

Now tow'rd the Tents awhile we journey'd on
With wary Pace, then lighted on the Ground,
Befriended by the Stars, that shimm'ring shone,
And Fires, that cast a trembling Gleam around.

With hasty Foot we press'd the dewy Sod,
Fit Answer making to each station'd Guard;
When full before us, as we onward trod,
A martial Form our further Progress barr'd.

He seem'd as tho' he there did list'ning stand,
His Face deep-muffled in his folded Cloak
Now threw it wide, snatch'd quick my dubious Hand,
And to a neighb'ring Tent his Speed betook.

With glowing Crimson the Pavilion shone,
Reflected by the lofty Taper's Ray,
The polish'd Armour, bright and deft to don,
Beside the royal Couch in order lay.

The Crown imperial glitter'd in mine Eye,
With various Gems magnificently grac'd,
Nigh which, as meant to guard its dignity,
A weighty Curtelax unsheath'd was plac'd.

The Chief unbonnetted, and drew me nigh,
Wrapt in a deepen'd Gloom his Face appear'd,
Like the dark Low'rings of the clouded Sky,
Ere the big-bursting Tempest's Voice is heard.

Revenge, Impatience, all that mads the Soul,
All that Despair and Frenzy's Flame inspires,
Shewn by the Tapers, in his Eyes did roll,
Hot meteors they amid the lesser Fires.

Tho' each dark Line I could not truly scan,
Yet thro' the Veil of his distemper'd Mein,
Broke forth a Likeness of that lofty Man,
Whom, whilom, at the Palace I had seen.

To quell his Feelings huge he sternly try'd,
Holding strong Combat with his fighting Soul,
Cresting himself with more than earthly Pride,
As tho' from Pow'r Supreme he scorn'd Controul.

At length (in Part subdu'd his troubled Breast)
On my impatient Ear these Accents broke,
(I pale and trembling as th' attentive Priest,
Who waits th' Inspirings of his mystic Oak!)

'Wonder no more why thou art hither brought,
The Secret of thy Birth shall now be shewn;
With glorious Ardour be thy Bosom fraught,
For know, thou art imperial RICHARD's Son.'

'Thy Father I, who fold thee in my Arms,
Thou royal Issue of PLANTAGENET!
Soon as my Pow'r hath quell'd these loud Alarms,
Thou shalt be known, be honour'd, and be great.'

'Rise from the Ground, and dry thy flowing Tears,
To Nature's Dues be other Hours assign'd!
Beset with Foes, Solicitude, and Cares,
Far other Thoughts must now possess the Mind.'

'To-morrow, Boy, I combat for my Crown,
To shield from Soil my Dignity and Fame:
Presumptuous RICHMOND seeks to win Renown,
And on my Ruin raise his upstart Name,'

'He leads yon shallow renegado Band,
Strangers to War and hazardous Emprize,
And 'gainst the mighty Chieftains of the Land,
Vain and unskill'd, a desp'rate Conflict tries.'

'Yet since Assurance is not giv'n to Man,
Nor can ev'n Kings command th' Event of War,
Since peevish Chance can foil the subtlest Plan
Of human Skill, and hurl our Schemes in Air.'

'To-morrow's Sun beholds me Conqueror,
Or sees me low among the Slaughter'd lie;
RICHARD shall never grace a Victor's Car,
But glorious win the Field, or glorious die.'

165

'But thou, my Son, heed and obey my Word;
Seek not to mingle in the wild Affray:
Far from the wing'd Shaft and gleaming Sword,
Patient await the Issue of the Day.'

'North of our Camp there stands a rising Mound,
(Thy Guide awaits to lead thee on the Way,)
Thence shalt thou rule the Prospect wide around,
And View each Chance, each movement of the Fray.'

'If righteous Fate to me the Conquest yield,
Then shall thy noble Birth to all be known;
Then boldly seek the Centre of the Field,
And midst my laurell'd Bands my Son I'll own.'

'But if blind Chance, that feld' determines right,
Rob me at once of Empire and Renown,
Be sure thy Father's Eyes are clos'd in Night,
Life were Disgrace when Chance had reft my Crown.'

'No means are left thee then, but instant Flight,
In dark Concealment must thou veil thy Head;
On RICHARD's Friends their fellest Rage and Spite
His Foes will wreak, and fear ev'n RICHARD dead.'

'Begone, my Son! This one Embrace! Away!
Some short Reflections claims this awful Night:
Ere from the East peep forth the glimm'ring Day,
My Knights attend to arm me for the Fight.'

Once more I knelt, he clasp'd my lifted Hands,
Bless'd me, and seem'd to check a struggling Tear;
Then led me forth to follow his Commands,
O'erwhelm'd with tenderest Grief, Suspense, and Fear.

What Need of more? Who knows not the Event
Of that dread Day, that desp'rate-foughten Field,
Where, with his wond'rous Deeds and Prowess spent,
By Numbers overpow'r'd, my Sire was kill'd?

A Son no more, what Course was left to tread,
To whom apply, or whither should I wend?
Back to my Tutor's Roof, by Instinct led,
My Orphan Footsteps did I pensive bend

O'er-ruling Fate against my Wishes wrought;
The pious Man, snatch'd from this frail Abode,
Had found the Blessing he so long had sought,
The Way to Immortality and God.

With flowing Eyes I left the sacred Door,
And with relying Heart to Heav'n did bend;
To God my Supplication did I pour,
To God, the Mourner's best and surest Friend,

That *He* would guide me to some safe Retreat,
Where daily Toil my daily Bread might earn,
Where pious Peace might soothe Ambition's Heat,
And my taught Heart sublimer Ardor learn.

He heard me – All I ask'd in thee was lent,
Thou lib'ral Proxy of my gracious God!
Thou paid'st my Industry with rich Content,
And giv'st my weary Age this soft Abode.

*The work is done, the Structure is compleat –*
*Long may the Produce of my humble Toil*
*Un-injur'd stand! and Echo long repeat,*
*Round the dear Walls,* Benevolence and MOYLE!

167

Hull refers near the end (p. 29) to the entry in the Eastwell parish register and says that 'this last Piece of Intelligence was transmitted to the Editor by a very sensible and worthy Clergyman now living, who kindly went from *Wye* to *Eastwell*, to collect as many Circumstances as he could, to confirm the Authenticity of this singular Story. To the Transcript of the Register he subjoined as follows:

It is observable that in the old Register there is prefixed to the Name of every Person of *noble Blood* such a Mark as this, ⌄⎯. At the Name of RICHARD PLANTAGENET there is the same Mark, (and it is the First that is so distinguished) only with this Difference, that there is a Line run across it, thus, ⌄⟋.

The Editor conjectures the Line, which is mentioned to run across the Mark of Nobility, to be what is stiled in Heraldry, the *Bar of Bastardy*.[1]

The Editor of this Poem holds it incumbent on him to return his most grateful Thanks to the Gentleman who sent him these curious Particulars, for the Trouble he took, and the Politeness of his Letter; the whole of which he should be proud to make publick, together with the Name, could he presume such a Liberty to be warrantable.

The clergyman who went 'from Wye to Eastwell' sounds suspiciously like Dr Brett, but he had died in 1744. The probable origin of the 'royal mark', which hardly resembles that shown here, has already been noticed (see Chapter Two); it may, in fact, be no more than a symbol that the copyist used to record his interest, with a line subsequently drawn through it to indicate that his abstract of that particular entry was complete!

# APPENDIX TWO

# *Some Journalistic Asides*

THE RELIABILITY OF DR BRETT'S STORY

Dr Brett's account of Richard Plantagenet as recorded by Peck was reprinted in volume 37 of the *Gentleman's Magazine* in June 1767. It was subsequently alleged that the story had been concocted by Brett and Dr Warren for their own amusement (presumably to deceive Peck, who was then compiling his *Desiderata Curiosa*), but other correspondents rushed to their defence.

SIR,

THE anecdote concerning *Richard Plantagenet*, natural son of our king *Richard* III. reprinted in your last Magazine from Mr *Peck's Desiderata Curiosa*, I observe, has been from thence republished in some of the evening papers. A gentleman, however, who signs (himself) R. T. in the St *James*'s chronicle of *August* 8, seems to entertain some doubt concerning the authenticity of that story, for he says 'At that time (that is, when the *Desiderata Curiosa* were published) I was informed that there was not the least foundation for the story, the whole being forged with a view to impose upon the credulity of Mr *Peck*, by a person who certainly succeeded, if that was his design.' Now Sir, Dr *Thomas Brett* of *Spring-Grove*, near *Eastwell*, was the person that penned the story, or that first put down the traditionary account in writing, with a view of obliging his countryman, Dr *William Warren*,

169

who was then fellow of *Trinity* hall, *Cambridge*, and there resident. Dr *Brett* and Dr *Warren*, both of whom I well know, were very serious men, and incapable of forming a design of imposing upon any body, in a point of history especially, and this is no more than a piece of justice which I owe to their irreproachable characters. The gentleman goes on 'the truth of the relation may be easily established, or refuted, by searching into the register of *Eastwell*; and therefore if any of your correspondents will give themselves the trouble of enquiring into the reality of this strange and improbable story, it will be esteemed a particular favour by your constant reader, &c.' If by the *reality of the story*, he means the whole of the ancedote, I profess I can neither give, nor procure any further account of *Richard Plantagenet* than what Dr *Brett* has given, the parties being long since dead; and can only say, that when I lived in the neighbourhood of *Eastwell*, which I did many years, the tradition very currently ran, as the doctor has delivered it; but if R. T. will be content with a literal extract from the old register of *Eastwell*, concerning the person in question, I am ready to oblige him in that, by assuring him, that I copied *verbatim*, above thirty years ago the following entry from thence.

'*Richard Plantagenet* was buryed the 22th daye of *Desember anno ut Supra*.' i.e. 1550.

All I shall farther say, is, and this I think may give some satisfaction, that *Richard* III. *certainly* had a *bastard* son of the name of *Richard*, see Mr *Drake's Eboracum* p. 117, where you will find, that he was knighted, when a youth, by his father, at *York*.

I *am, SIR, yours,*
T. ROW.[1]

The writer is mistaken in this last assertion. Sir George Buck had said that '[the king] made Richard of Gloucester, his base son [Captain of] Calais' in September 1483 and perhaps knighted him, but a later grant makes it clear that this was, in fact, *John* of Gloucester, and not Richard. (See P.W. Hammond, 'The Illegitimate Children of Richard III', in J. Petre (ed.), *Richard III: Crown and People* (Gloucester, 1985), p. 18.) Nevertheless, there is no reason to doubt Mr Row's main argument, which received further support from a gentleman signing himself 'Verus' in a subsequent edition.

Mr URBAN,

SEEING an attempt in your Magazine (p. 457.) to invalidate the account of *Richard Plantagenet*, and happening, at the same time, to be in the company of several gentlemen of capacity and integrity, well acquainted with *Eastwell*, I can assure you that the story, as related by *Peck*, is here universally credited; and that the well which *Richard* sunk for his use near his little dwelling-house is always shewn as a great curiosity to strangers.                    *I am, Yours, &c.*
     *Hythe, Oct. 5, 1767.*                              VERUS

RICHARD'S SUPPOSED 'AUTOBIOGRAPHY'

This was first noticed in a letter submitted to *Notes and Queries*, 4th series, 6 ( 31 December 1870), p. 567.

MS AUTOBIOGRAPHY OF THE NATURAL SON OF KING RICHARD III. – It is stated in a book entitled *The Portfolio*, which I sometimes take up as a relaxation from graver studies, that this person, who, as tradition reports, was buried at Eastwell in Kent, was employed by Sir Edward Dering of Surrenden to superintend certain repairs going on at his house, and that he (Sir Edward) became so much interested in him as, when the work was completed, to have allowed him the use of a house on his estate, which he continued to occupy till the time of his death. During this time, it appears, he composed a history of his life, and put it into the hands of his patron and benefactor, with a request not to 'read it till after his decease'. He soon after died, and the aforesaid manuscript (inclosed, as it is supposed, by his friend within the wall) 'was not known nor discovered till so lately as 1787. It is now in the possession of the family of the Derings.'

The last statement I find to be incorrect, being informed by the present worthy baronet that he knows nothing of the manuscript, and that probably it was lost to its former possessors hard upon sixty years ago.

I wish to inquire if anything is known of this interesting document, which might possibly throw some light upon the character and life, private and public, of one of the most extraordinary and most unpopular of England's kings.

EDMUND TEW, M.A.

Patching Rectory, Arundel.

Richard clearly could not have died in two different places, and the only reasonable conclusion is that the story told of Sir Thomas Moyle had become associated with – or had been appropriated by – the Dering family. It may not be without significance that a later Sir Edward Dering, who died in 1644, 'invented for himself a Saxon pedigree, interpolated the name and arms of a fictitious ancestor into ancient rolls of arms which belonged to him and set up pseudo-ancestral brasses in Pluckley church'.[2] Subsequent correspondents expressed reservations about *The Portfolio*, which was not to be found in the British Museum, and suggested that William Heseltine's 1829 novel *The Last of the Plantagenets* was responsible for the belief that the old bricklayer had committed the story of his life to paper because it was written in an autobiographical style. A Mr D.J. Stewart wrote to one of the enquirers, Miss R.H.

Busk, pointing out that 'the first printed edition of Horace with date was in 1474' and asking if there had been time for the book to have become well known in England when Richard was allegedly introduced to it. However, Miss Busk thought that its rarity would have caused him to prize it, perhaps more so if it was his schoolmaster's parting gift (*Notes and Queries*, 6th series, 9 (5 January 1884)).

MISS KELLY AND RICHARD PLANTAGENET

What follows is part of an unsigned article that appeared in *Kent Life* in August 1964, p. 70. On one level it is a fairly typical modern retelling of the legend of Richard of Eastwell (complete with misunderstandings), but it testifies to its continuing fascination and how it has helped to save part of the church for posterity. If it can inspire and encourage interest in the ruins, then it clearly still matters, even today.

Miss Mary Wentworth Kelly is one woman with a definite answer to the question which is perplexing a good many, 'What really can be done to preserve our heritage of 15,000 medieval churches?'

The doubters point out that this is an average of one lovely old church for every 3,000 people, even if the churches were still close to big centres of population.

To which Miss Kelly replies, 'It is just a matter of getting down to a little work.'

She is putting her teaching into effect at Eastwell, near Ashford, at the famous old Pilgrims' church in Eastwell Park, which had been lying in unsightly ruins since 1950.

Eastwell is the home of one of Kent's legends.

There have been a number of big houses on the site in the park now occupied by Eastwell Towers. The last but one was a favourite shooting box of King Edward VII, and Queen

Marie of Romania was born there. One of the earlier houses was built for Sir Thomas Moyle in the 1500's.

After its completion, a man was buried in Eastwell Church and his name was entered in the parish register as Richard Plantagenet. That was on December 22, 1550.

So much is fact.

The legend is that Richard was a natural son of Richard III. His identity was discovered when the builder of the house for Sir Thomas found one of his masons, an elderly quiet man, reading a Latin book.

Such an accomplishment was so rare that he pressed the old man for his story. Reluctantly the mason told it.

He had always known there was something different about him when he was a boy. He was brought up expensively but almost secretly.

Then one night he was roused from his sleep and taken on a long journey. In a tent he was brought before a richly dressed man. The man told the boy he was his father.

'Tomorrow,' he said, 'I fight a battle. If I win, one day you will be King of England. If I lose, hide yourself for they will try to kill you.'

That night was the eve of Bosworth Field. Richard lost his life. The Plantagenet line was ended and the boy had minded his father's advice ever since.

And as Miss Kelly says, 'That is a story which will live for ever because it must always remain a mystery.'

Miss Kelly, born in Australia, but whose mother came from East Sussex, is a medievalist, and fell in love with the old church by Eastwell Lake long before the war when she used to come to Kent on archaeological work in her Austin 'Seven'.

During the war, Eastwell was used by the army as a tank testing centre and the church fell out of use. One anti-aircraft shell went right through the tower and possibly the structure was weakened by other gunfire.

In 1950, a few days after 150 people had gathered in the church for a funeral, the roof fell in. Piles of rubble were taken away for road-making, the wonderfully carved poppy-head pews were burned because no-one would buy them. Stained glass and the rood screen vanished and is believed now to be as far away as York and Devon.

When Miss Kelly saw the ruins, she was horrified.

'Luckily, I am a little better off now,' she said, 'and I was able to try to do something about it.'

Week after week she and women friends, interested in archaeology, came down from London in her Rolls-Royce, to dig out the shoulder-high nettles and to carry out debris from the old nave. The vicar, the Rev. P. Stearns, and parishioners headed by Mr. D.G.S. Winters, who had separately been making plans, joined them in the labour.

Now the ruins stand clear and tidy, and the floor of the nave is an open space. It is planned to turf this over.

The legendary site of the tomb of Richard Plantagenet in the south wall has been grouted with concrete and a plaque fixed.

To mark the end of the work, Miss Kelly planted half-a-dozen each of white roses (for York), rosemary (for remembrance) and broom (the Latin name of broom is Planta Genista and from this the Plantagenets get both their name and their heraldic device).

The next part of Miss Kelly's task is to help the vicar in his plans to make all the church site into a garden leading down to the lake.

'And I very much would like to do something about the wonderful Moyle and Finch tombs,' she said. A brick building with a concrete roof has been built over them but there is so much condensation that very soon the tombs will decay. I would like to see another protective cover put up with windows so that visitors could see the tombs. That

Members of the Richard III Society visit 'Richard Plantagenet's grave', *c.* 1964.

would cost about £4,000 and I am not sure that I can afford it myself.'

She is also planning to give up her Sloane Street flat to come down to live near the church.

# APPENDIX THREE

## *The Hopper Ring*

The Hopper ring is made of silver, and has a central ornament which bears traces of enamel and contains a small piece of wood said to be a fragment of the 'True Cross'. It is inscribed '*MKENI*' and '*IESVS*', and may have been brought to England at the time of the Crusades. The sacred wood would have been regarded as a talisman, and may be the origin of the expression to 'touch wood' (for luck).

The ring first came to public attention when the architect Thomas Hopper died aged 81 on 11 August 1856. His obituary in the *Illustrated London News* was concerned mainly with the many buildings he had designed for worthy individuals and institutions, but also noted that 'there exists a most curious tradition in his family that they are descended from a natural daughter of Richard III, by a lady the King brought with him from Edinburgh to Dover'.[1] The lady and her daughter were both called Ann, and the girl married a wealthy yeoman miller named Hopper whose mill was in Canterbury. King Richard allegedly gave the ring to one of them (perhaps to the daughter

The Hopper Ring, drawn by Geoffrey Wheeler.

as a wedding gift?), and their descendants treasured it for nearly four centuries. It has been suggested that the inscription should begin with *IESVS*, in which case it would read 'Jesus knows me' in the Scots – an intriguing possibility given the alleged recipient's known Scottish links.

What, then, are we to make of this? Some writers assume that 'Richard of Eastwell' was Richard of Gloucester's son by this lady, and postulate that if the boy was really 15 or 16 in 1485 then Gloucester must have been in Edinburgh in 1468 or 1469.[2] But there is no evidence for this ('Ann' has probably been confused with the 'lady of quality' mentioned by *The Parallel*), and the only time he indisputably visited the city was when he briefly captured it in July 1482. It would not be surprising if he began a liaison with 'Mistress Ann' during his lengthy absence from Middleham, kept her with him when he retired to Berwick, and decided to provide for her when he learned she was pregnant. He was constable of Dover Castle *c.*1481–3, but there is no obvious reason why a place so far from Scotland should have become her new home. The only logical explanation is that the journey was made by sea rather than by land, partly, perhaps, to keep the matter well away from Richard's wife, Anne Neville. The name Hopper occurs frequently in Canterbury Archdeaconry Court wills from 1449 onwards, and a Hopper Mill (and field), operated by one John Hopper between 1547 and 1585, existed in Canterbury until it burned down in 1934. Richard is said to have made a written promise to ennoble Ann Hopper's children, but the documents were burned by Thomas Hopper's father 'in a fit of drunken spleen'.[3] This is not altogether improbable, since an obituary in *The Builder*, 14 (1856), p. 14, noted that the elder Hopper's 'intemperate habits' had obliged his son to assist in 'or rather carry on' his father's business from the age of 18.[4]

On Thomas Hopper's death the ring passed to Jessalina, his youngest daughter, and then to her daughter Emily Euphemia.

The story is told of how, one day, a London lawyer was examining the possessions of one of his clients, an elderly gentleman, when he came across the ring and was told he could throw it away! The lawyer asked if he might keep it, and loaned it to Mr Clarence Daniel, who placed it in his private museum at Eyam in Derbyshire.[5] When Mr Daniel died in 1987, Mrs Audrey Cartwright of the Richard III Society suggested to his widow and to Dr J.S. Beck (the then owner) that it deserved to be seen more widely, and they agreed to allow the Society to place it on display at Warwick Castle. It was exhibited at Warwick for five years before being returned to Eyam in May 1996.

Family traditions are almost impossible to 'prove' even if (as must usually be the case) they are based on *something*, and this is no less true of this story than it is of others; but there is no discernible connection with Richard of York or Richard of Eastwell except that Eastwell is just over 12 miles from Canterbury and 25 from Dover. There is no particular reason why Richard should have been aware of Ann of Edinburgh's existence, but if he was (and if, as we surmise, she was approximately ten years younger), by 1541 she would have been his only surviving first cousin. It is perhaps just possible that a family link with the area persuaded Richard to go there after leaving St John's at the Dissolution, but the details we have are so sketchy that it is difficult to pursue the matter further. Enquiries made at Dover Castle in the 1980s yielded nothing, and all we are left with are suggestions that may, or may not, have anything to commend them. The late Joyce Rossall thought that the lady could have been a member of the Boyd family, forced into exile when the young Scottish king James III asserted his independence in 1469; but this date, we have assumed, is too early for Richard of Gloucester's liaison. Another suggestion is that she was connected with Lennoxlove (or, more precisely, with the fortified tower that stood there in the late fifteenth century), and was perhaps a gentlewoman in the service of the Maitland family who occupied it.[6] Richard's camp was located at nearby Belvedere,[7] and he could well have formed such an attachment while he was in the area. It is also interesting that, after he became king, he proposed a marriage between one of James's sons and his niece, a daughter of the Duke and Duchess of Suffolk, who was also called Anne, but whether this Anne has in some way lent her name to the story is now quite impossible to say.

# A Note for Visitors to
# St Mary's Church, Eastwell

St Mary's Church is not signposted, so visitors may find the following note useful:

Leave the A251 Challock–Ashford road at Sandyhurst Lane (just north of Kennington) and turn right into Lenacre Street after passing the magnificent Towers (built in 1843) on your right. Continue until you reach a right turn, which will bring you to the church. There is ample parking adjacent to the church tower on your left.

Alternatively, park next to the green at Boughton Aluph and join the North Downs Way (F.P. 214) just beyond St Christopher's church. Walk diagonally across the park, crossing the road leading to the hotel en route, until you reach a barbed-wire fence. Turn right, keeping the fence on your left, and after a short distance join a metalled road, which approaches from the right. Continue along this, and you will soon see the ruins of St Mary's on your left. Turn left immediately past a large rhododendron hedge on your left.

# Notes

1. A more extreme example is *The Princes in the Tower* by Elizabeth Jenkins, where the future Edward V is not even born until page 65!

2. For a discussion of this problem see D. Baldwin, *Elizabeth Woodville: Mother of the Princes in the Tower* (Stroud, 2002), appendix 5.

3. *The Crowland Chronicle Continuations 1459–1486*, ed. N. Pronay and J. Cox (1986), p. 163.

4. A. Hanham, *Richard III and his Early Historians 1483–1535* (Oxford, 1975), pp. 94–5.

5. Quoted in *The Anglica Historia of Polydore Vergil 1485–1537*, ed. D. Hay (Camden Society, 1950), p. xxviii.

6. *Three Books of Polydore Vergil's English History*, ed. H. Ellis (Camden Society, 1844), p. 188.

7. Thomas More, who tells the same story albeit more elaborately, says that Tyrell's confession was the source of his information.

8. Vergil, *English History*, p. 188.

9. Dominic Mancini, *The Usurpation of Richard III*, trans. C.A.J. Armstrong (Oxford, 1969; repr. Gloucester, 1984), p. 93.

10. *Ibid.*, p. 93.

11. *More's History of King Richard III*, ed. J.R. Lumby (Cambridge, 1883), p. 81.

12. *Ibid.*, p. 84.

13. Thomas More, *The History of King Richard III*, ed. R.S. Sylvester (New Haven, 1976), p. xv.

14. These references are conveniently brought together in K. Dockray, *Richard III: A Source Book* (Stroud, 1997), pp. 77–9, except for MS Ashmole 1448.60, which is noticed in P.M. Kendall, *Richard III* (1973), p. 411, and the *Divisie Chronicle*, which may be found in M. Lulofs, 'Richard III: Dutch Sources', *The Ricardian*, 3 (1974), p. 13.

15. *The Great Chronicle of London*, ed. A.H. Thomas and I.D. Thornley (1938; repr. Gloucester, 1983), pp. 234, 236–7.

16. More, *History*, p. 80.

17. *British Library Harleian Manuscript 433*, ed. R. Horrox and P.W. Hammond, 4 vols (Upminster and London, 1979–83), vol. 2, p. 211; vol. 3, p. 114.

18. A. Williamson, *The Mystery of the Princes* (Dursley, 1978), pp. 122–3.

19. These are only some of Mr Leslau's covert rebuses or hidden meanings. For a useful summary see G. Norman, 'How Holbein Hid a Royal Secret', *The Times*, Friday 25 March 1983, p. 12.

20. A.J. Pollard, *Richard III and the Princes in the Tower* (Stroud, 1991), p. 132.

21. It has been pointed out that Clement apparently joined Henry VIII and other noblemen at a feat of arms held on 1 June 1510, that an entry in the Louvain register dated 1562 describes him as 'Dominus Joannes Clemens, nobilis, Anglus', and that he was buried near the Cathedral's high altar in a place usually reserved for the greatest in society. But if it was generally known that he was Prince Richard, why bother to call him Clement at all? See T. Merriam, 'John Clement: His Identity and his Marshfoot House in Essex', *Moreana*, 25 (1988), pp. 145–52.

22. More, *History*, p. 84.
23. B. Fields, *Royal Blood* (New York, 1998), p. 247.
24. See D.M. Kleyn, *Richard of England* (1990), and Ann Wroe, 'From Ann Wroe', in 'Who Was Perkin Warbeck', *Ricardian Bulletin* (Summer 2005), pp. 24–6.
25. Perkin's letter to Isabella has been printed by F. Madden, 'Documents Relating to Perkin Warbeck, with Remarks on his History', *Archaeologia*, 27 (1838), pp. 199–200. His letter to his mother and his confession may be found in A.F. Pollard, *The Reign of Henry VII from Contemporary Sources*, 3 vols (1913–14), vol. i, pp. 172–3, 183–5, and his speech to King James in Francis Bacon, *The History of the Reign of King Henry VII*, ed. R. Lockyer (1971), p. 160.
26. They mocked Warbeck's claims in public while referring to him as the Duke of York in private – but this may, as Ann Wroe points out, have been simply the name by which he was known. *Perkin: A Story of Deception* (2004), p. 214.
27. Quoted by Wroe in *Perkin*, p. 525.
28. A suggestion also made by Ian Arthurson, 'Perkin Warbeck and the Murder of the Princes in the Tower', in M. Aston and R. Horrox (eds), *Much Heaving and Shoving: Essays for Colin Richmond* (2005), pp. 158–66.
29. G. Smith 'Lambert Simnel and the King from Dublin', *The Ricardian*, 10 (1996), pp. 498–536.
30. The fact that Simnel was shown to the people on the shoulders of Great Darcy of Platen at his coronation would imply that he was 10 rather than 15. Mr Smith does not mention this.
31. Sir George Buck refers to a plot by Morton and 'a certain countess' (presumably Henry Tudor's mother Margaret Beaufort) to poison the two princes that he had seen mentioned in 'an old manuscript book', now lost. But

Morton spent the whole of Richard III's reign first in custody then in exile, and may have been credited with more influence than he really had. Buck, *The History of King Richard the Third*, ed. A.N. Kincaid (Gloucester, 1979), p. cxii.

32. J. Dening, *Secret History: The Truth about Richard III and the Princes* (Brandon, 1996), p. 82. Morton is described by Thomas More as 'of a meane stature' (*Utopia*, ed. J.R. Lumby (Cambridge, 1908), p. 27).

33. Dening, *Secret History*, pp. 45, 65.

34. Vergil, *Anglica Historia*, ed. Hay, p. 13 n.

35. Bacon, *Henry VII*, p. 54.

CHAPTER TWO. RICHARD OF EASTWELL

1. See C. Igglesden, *A Saunter through Kent with Pen and Pencil*, vol. 3 (Ashford, 1901).

2. 'Hugh de Montfort holds a manor, EASTWELL, which Frederick held from King Edward. It answers for 1 sulung [nominally 160 acres]'. *Domesday Book. Kent*, ed. P. Morgan (Chichester, 1983), Sect. 9, entry 1.

3. Michael, the first baron, distinguished himself at Crecy; his younger son Richard, the third of the line, accompanied John of Gaunt to Spain in 1386 and died there; and Robert, the fourth and last baron Poynings, fought at Verneuil in 1424, five years before his son and heir apparent, Sir Richard, was killed near Orleans. Service was not without meaning in those days. G.E.C. *et al.*, *The Complete Peerage*, 12 vols (1910–59), vol. 10, pp. 660–5.

4. Igglesden, *A Saunter through Kent*, pp. 14, 17. Some of this information is taken from C.R. Councer, 'The Medieval and Renaissance Painted Glass of Eastwell', *Archaeologia Cantiana*, 59 (1946), pp. 109–13.

5. A. Weir, *The Princes in the Tower* (1992), p. 176. P.G. Dormer, *Eastwell Park Historiette* (Eastwell Park, 1999), p. 31.

6. This unfortunate lady suffered from kleptomania (a recurrent urge to steal) and is said to have been accompanied on her travels by servants who replaced items she had pilfered. She died in 1848 at the early age of 39.

7. These particulars are based upon E.W. Parkin, 'The Vanishing Houses of Kent. 8. Lake House, Eastwell', *Archaeologia Cantiana*, 83 (1968), pp. 151–61.

8. F. Peck, *Desiderata Curiosa*, vol. 2 (1779), pp. 249–51. Spelling modernised. There is one anachronism in that the 'so-called Garter star (allegedly worn by Richard III) originated at a chapter held on April 27 1626, when knight companions were required, whenever they were not wearing the robes of the Order, to wear upon the left side of their coats or cloaks, the badge of the Order, the cross of St George, encircled with the Garter' (P. J. Begent and H. Chesshyre, *The Most Noble Order of the Garter: 650 Years* (1999), p. 70). I am indebted to Geoffrey Wheeler for this reference.

9. This was certainly the case at Kirby Muxloe, built in the same style by William, Lord Hastings, in the early 1480s, where the three senior craftsmen each received 8*d* per day. A.H. Thompson (ed., with an introduction and notes), 'The Building Accounts of Kirby Muxloe Castle 1480–1484', *Transactions of the Leicestershire Archaeological Society*, 11 (1915).

10. R.H. D'Elboux, 'Some Kentish Indents', *Archaeologia Cantiana*, 59 (1946), pp. 98–9. P.W. Hammond, 'The Illegitimate Children of Richard III', in J. Petre (ed.), *Richard III, Crown and People* (Gloucester, 1985), p. 21.

11. *More's History of King Richard III*, ed. J.R. Lumby (Cambridge, 1883), p. 2.

12. King Richard was still only 30 in September 1483, so John cannot have been much more than 14. Professor Hicks notes that Richard visited Pontefract (Pomfret) on several occasions in 1473–4 and suggests that his son may have been conceived then – making him only 8 or 9 when his father became king. M. Hicks, *Anne Neville: Queen to Richard III* (Stroud, 2006), pp. 157–8.

13. Peck, *Desiderata Curiosa*, vol. 2, pp. 250–1. There was also a local legend (first noticed in John Throsby's *Select Views in Leicestershire* in 1789) that a young man who was believed to be a son of King Richard acted as an ostler to the King's horses at Bosworth, and was befriended and hidden by a local blacksmith after the battle. He is said to have learned the trade and to have worked as a blacksmith in either Earl Shilton or Bosworth; but we are not told his name and the story may be no more than a mangled, half-remembered, version of Dr Brett's account. I am indebted to Geoffrey Wheeler for referring me to R.C. Bishop, 'Richard Plantagenet of Eastwell – Fact or Fiction', *The Ricardian*, 3 (1974).

14. Igglesden, *A Saunter through Kent*, p. 21.

15. *Ibid.*, p. 23.

16. *Ibid.*, p. 10.

17. *Ibid.*, p. 16.

18. D'Elboux, 'Some Kentish Indents', p. 96.

19. J.C. Wedgwood (*History of Parliament*, vol. 1, *Biographies* (1936), p. 617) could find no trace of him after 1471, but his last will is dated 11 December 1479 (D'Elboux, 'Some Kentish Indents', p. 99). Sir Thomas Moyle was the third son of Sir Walter's eldest son, John.

20. Peck, *Desiderata Curiosa*, vol. 2, p. 250.

21. D'Elboux, 'Some Kentish Indents', p. 98.

CHAPTER THREE. RICHARD OF YORK

1. The Taylor MSS, quoted in T. Auden, *Shrewsbury: A Historical and Topographical Account of the Town* (1905), p. 111.
2. These particulars are taken from J. Leland, *De Rebus Britannicis Collectanea*, ed. T. Hearne, 6 vols (1770), vol. 4, pp. 179–84.
3. S. Bentley (ed.), *Excerpta Historica or Illustrations of English History* (1831), pp. 242–3. C.L. Scofield, *The Life and Reign of Edward the Fourth*, 2 vols (1923), vol. 2, p. 94.
4. Bentley (ed.), *Excerpta Historica*, pp. 366–79. M. Hicks, *Edward V: The Prince in the Tower* (Stroud, 2003), pp. 127–8.
5. *Calendar of the Close Rolls, Edward IV, Edward V, Richard III, 1476–1485* (1954), p. 1.
6. A.R. Myers (ed.), *The Household of Edward IV: The Black Book and the Ordinance of 1478* (Manchester, 1959), pp. 223, 268 n.
7. See A. Alles, 'Heraldry in Medieval England', in P. Coss and M. Keen (eds), *Heraldry, Pageantry and Social Display in Medieval England* (2002), pp. 97–8. I am indebted to Geoffrey Wheeler for this reference.
8. 'Livery' in this context consisted of bread and ale for a bedtime snack and, from All Hallows day to Good Friday, the 'winter livery' of candles and firewood. See P.M. Kendall, *Richard III* (1973), pp. 47, 442 n. 7.
9. J.O. Halliwell (ed.), *Letters of the Kings of England*, 2 vols (1846), vol. 1, pp. 137–9, slightly amended in R. Steele (ed.), *Kings' Letters* (1903), pp. 240–2.
10. Quoted in A. Wroe, *Perkin: A Story of Deception* (2004), p. 525.
11. The figures were damaged by the Puritan iconoclast Richard Culmer in 1543. Bernard Rackham (*The Ancient

*Glass of Canterbury Cathedral* (1949)) notes that only the King and Queen retain their original heads. See F. Hepburn, *Portraits of the Later Plantagenets* (1986), pp. 57–8.

12. 'Narrative of the Marriage of Richard Duke of York with Anne of Norfolk: The Matrimonial Feast and the Grand Jousting', in W.H. Black (ed.), *Illustrations of Ancient State and Chivalry from manuscripts Preserved in the Ashmolean Museum* (Roxburghe Club, 1840), pp. 28–31.

13. I am indebted for these last thoughts to Ann Wroe, *Perkin*, p. 62.

14. A. Crawford, 'The Mowbray Inheritance', in J. Petre (ed.), *Richard III: Crown and People* (Gloucester, 1985), pp. 79–85.

15. Scofield, *Edward the Fourth*, vol. 2, p. 323.

16. *Calendar of the Patent Rolls, Edward IV, Edward V, Richard III, 1476–1485* (1901), pp. 153, 230, 330. He was appointed lord lieutenant of Ireland in May 1479, and the appointment was renewed for a further twelve years the following year.

17. The word apparently referred to the material rather than to the colour of it, although this is not precluded. See N.H. Nicolas, *Privy Purse Expenses of Elizabeth of York: Wardrobe Accounts of Edward IV* (1830), p. 255.

18. *Ibid.*, pp. 155–6, 160–1.

19. Richard III said that Dorset, 'not fearing God, nor the peril of his soul, hath many and sundry maids, widows, and wives damnably and without shame devoured, deflowered, and defouled' (*Cal. Pat. Rolls, 1476–85*, p. 371). He may have exaggerated, but Dorset undoubtedly 'enjoyed' a reputation of this sort.

20. *The Crowland Chronicle Continuations 1459–1486*, ed. N. Pronay and J. Cox (1986), p. 149.

CHAPTER FOUR. UNCLE RICHARD

1. *An English Chronicle of the Reigns of Richard II, Henry IV, Henry V, and Henry VI*, ed. J.S. Davies (Camden Society, 1856), p. 83.
2. It is not known when Richard entered, or left, Warwick's household. Professor Kendall and Miss Scofield favoured 1461/2–5 while Professor Ross and others have argued for (what seems to me) a comparatively late sojourn there between 1465 and 1468.
3. There is no evidence to support Kendall's suggestion that Elizabeth did her best to make 'the undersized lad from Yorkshire with the awkward torso and the solemn face' feel uncomfortable. P.M. Kendall, *Richard III* (1973), p. 61. For a more balanced view see D. Baldwin, *Elizabeth Woodville: Mother of the Princes in the Tower* (Stroud, 2002).
4. Rivers was disputing some lands in Norfolk with a certain Roger Townshend, and they agreed to submit their unresolved differences to Richard's arbitration. Rivers would hardly have done this if he had regarded the Duke as a personal enemy. C.E. Moreton, 'A Local Dispute and the Politics of 1483: Roger Townshend, Earl Rivers and the Duke of Gloucester', *The Ricardian*, 7 (1989), pp. 305–7.
5. John Warkworth, *A Chronicle of the First Thirteen Years of the Reign of King Edward the Fourth*, ed. J.O. Halliwell (Camden Society, 1839), p. 18. *Historie of the Arrivall of Edward IV in England and the Finall Recouerye of His Kingdomes from Henry VI, A.D. M.CCCC.LXXI*, ed. J. Bruce (Camden Society, 1846), p. 30. An illustrated contemporary French version of the *Arrival* does show the pinioned Prince being struck down in Edward IV's presence, however, and proves that the story of his murder was current on the Continent within a

short time of the battle being fought. A.F. Sutton and L. Visser-Fuchs, *Richard III's Books* (Stroud, 1997), plate ix.

6.  Warkworth, *Chronicle*, p. 21.
7.  *Historie of the Arrivall*, p. 38.
8.  *The Paston Letters A.D. 1422–1509*, ed. J. Gairdner, 6 vols (1904), vol. 5, pp. 135–6.
9.  *Ingulph's Chronicle of the Abbey of Croyland*, trans. H.T. Riley (1854), p. 470.
10. Professor Kendall suggests that Richard was moved mainly by concern for the girl he had known in his youth at Middleham, but it is perhaps more likely that, as Professor Hicks argues, his interest in her lands was always paramount. Kendall, *Richard III*, pp. 107–9. M. Hicks, *False, Fleeting, Perjur'd Clarence 1449–78* (Bangor, 1992), pp. 100–2.
11. *Paston Letters*, ed. Gairdner, vol. 5, p. 195.
12. *Rotuli Parliamentorum*, ed. J. Strachey *et al.*, 6 vols (1767–77), vol. 6, p. 100–1. It is unclear if the full dispensation was deliberately withheld by the papal penitentiary or not issued because of some misunderstanding or error.
13. M. Barnfield, 'Richard and Anne's Dispensation', *Ricardian Bulletin* (Spring 2006), pp. 30–2. The fullest study of the matter is by Professor Michael Hicks (*Anne Neville: Queen to Richard III* (Stroud, 2006), pp. 131–49), where it is suggested that the couple did not seek a second dispensation, notwithstanding the obvious threat to their son's legitimacy and his right to inherit.
14. *The Chronicles of the White Rose of York*, ed. J.C. Giles (1845), p. 28.
15. The sequence of events is fully described in Hicks, *Clarence*, pp. 119–27.
16. This had been said both of Edward and of other kings and senior members of the royal family who had been born

outside England, including Richard II and John of Gaunt. The theory has recently been revived by Dr Michael K. Jones (*Bosworth: Psychology of a Battle* (Stroud, 2002)), using a document kept in Rouen Cathedral that implies that Richard, Duke of York (Edward's father), was away on campaign when his son was conceived. Other writers have argued against this interpretation, but the crucial question is surely where was York's wife Cecily? If she went on the campaign with her husband (as medieval ladies were wont to do), the problem disappears.

17. Mancini wrote that Queen Elizabeth 'concluded that her offspring by the king would never come to the throne, unless the duke of Clarence were removed; and of this she easily persuaded the king'. 'At that time [he says] Richard duke of Gloucester was so overcome with grief . . . that he was overheard to say that he would one day avenge his brother's death,' but he benefited considerably from Clarence's fall and his protests, as Professor Hicks notes, ring hollow. Dominic Mancini, *The Usurpation of Richard III*, trans. C.A.J. Armstrong (Oxford, 1969; reprinted Gloucester, 1984), p. 63. Kendall, *Richard III*, p. 125. Hicks, *Clarence*, pp. 136–7. Hicks argues, convincingly, that Edward would not have taken such drastic action against his brother unless he knew that Richard approved.

18. Mancini, *Usurpation*, p. 71.

19. The precise sequence and location of these events is open to question – I have here followed Kendall (*Richard III*, pp. 173–8), who explains his reasons for preferring this interpretation in pp. 463–4 nn. 1, 2.

20. This section is based on M. Hicks, *Richard III* (Stroud, 2000), pp. 83–4. It is impossible to say if there would have been a reconciliation if Edward had lived longer, but Richard's accession meant that Oxford had little

alternative but to support Henry Tudor. Their final confrontation at Bosworth must have been personal as well as dynastic, and there is an element of natural justice in Oxford's (and Henry's) success.

21. Kendall, *Richard III*, p. 112. Similarly, he suspected no ulterior motive when Richard took the Countess of Warwick from Beaulieu to Middleham in 1473 (pp. 111–12).

CHAPTER FIVE. INTO THE TOWER

1. *Ingulph's Chronicle of the Abbey of Croyland*, trans. H.T. Riley (1854), p. 488.
2. *The Stonor Letters and Papers*, ed. C.L. Kingsford, 2 vols (Camden Society, 1919), vol. 2, p. 160.
3. R. Davies (ed.), *Extracts from the Municipal Records of the City of York during the Reigns of Edward IV. Edward V. and Richard III* (1843), p. 149.
4. *Ingulph's Chronicle*, p. 488.
5. *More's History of King Richard III*, ed. J.R. Lumby (Cambridge, 1883), p. 9.
6. Dominic Mancini, *The Usurpation of Richard III*, trans. C.A.J. Armstrong (Oxford, 1969; repr. Gloucester, 1984), p. 69.
7. Edward and Lady Butler were fifth cousins, so the King could have sought an annulment based on consanguinity had he thought it necessary. The legal position was that the marriage was permanently invalid if Elizabeth knew her husband was precontracted when she married him, but if she was unaware of it their union could have been formalised after Lady Butler's death.
8. More, *Richard III*, pp. 18, 45.
9. P.M. Kendall, *Richard III* (1973), p. 210.
10. More, *Richard III*, pp. 39–41.

11. It would be fascinating to know what Duchess Cecily thought of these insinuations. Remarkably, perhaps, she appears to have remained on good terms with her son Richard, and declared unequivocally that her husband was Edward IV's father when she made her will in 1495.

12. Mancini, *Usurpation*, p. 93.

13. *The Great Chronicle of London*, ed. A.H. Thomas and I.D. Thornley (1938; repr. Gloucester, 1983), p. 234.

14. *Ingulph's Chronicle*, p. 490.

15. C. Ross, *Richard III* (1981), p. 99.

16. *Ingulph's Chronicle*, p. 491.

17. *British Library Harleian Manuscript 433*, ed. R. Horrox and P.W. Hammond, 4 vols (Upminster and London, 1979–83), vol. 3, p. 190.

18. *Ingulph's Chronicle*, p. 496. Ross, *Richard III*, p. 101.

19. The agreement did not expressly state that Elizabeth would leave sanctuary herself, but this was surely part of the bargain? Perhaps, as Paul Murray Kendall suggests, 'she had secretly agreed to retire to a country house . . . where she could, in seclusion, support a modest state on her annuity of 700 marks' (*Richard III*, p. 287).

20. Vergil implies that her letter was sent soon after she had left sanctuary, but it may have been somewhat later and it did not, apparently, reach Dorset until after Henry and his followers had left Brittany for France in October 1484.

21. Elizabeth of York was sent to reside at Sheriff Hutton Castle and it is likely that other homes were found for Cecily, who would have been 15 in 1484, and Anne, who would have been 9. But Catherine and Bridget, the two youngest sisters, very probably remained with the Queen.

22. *British Library Harleian Manuscript*, vol. 1, p. 143.

23. The tradition is said to have originated 'well before the eighteenth century' (A. Williamson, *The Mystery of the Princes* (Dursley, 1978), p. 122). It may be worth noting

that Tyrell married a Cornish heiress, Anne, sole daughter of Sir John Arundel of Lanherne by his first wife Elizabeth. Sir John remarried after Elizabeth's death and had other children, one of whom, a daughter named Katherine, married (as her second husband) John Moyle of Eastwell, Sir Walter's son. See W.E. Hampton, 'Sir James Tyrell: With Some Notes of the Austin Friars London and those Buried there', in J. Petre (ed.), *Richard III, Crown and People* (Gloucester, 1985), p. 204.

24. *The Crowland Chronicle Continuations 1459–1486*, ed. N. Pronay and J. Cox (1986), p. 175.

25. *Ibid*. This might be taken to imply that Richard and Anne had not secured a full dispensation for their marriage after all.

26. Sir George Buck, *The History of King Richard the Third*, ed. A.N. Kincaid (Gloucester, 1979), p. 191.

27. See A. Hanham. 'Sir George Buck and Princess Elizabeth's Letter: A Problem in Detection', *The Ricardian*, 7 (1987), pp. 398–400.

28. I am indebted for these particulars to Livia Visser-Fuchs's excellent article 'Where did Elizabeth of York find Consolation?', *The Ricardian*, 9 (1993), pp. 469–70. The *Tristan* is British Library Harleian Manuscript 49, and the *Boethius* British Library Royal 20 A xix. Elizabeth signed the former at the foot of the page that has Richard's *ex libris*, but inscribed the latter unobtrusively on the end flyleaf.

29. *Ingulph's Chronicle*, p. 499.

30. William, Lord Hastings, had been Edward's original guardian, and his wardship, together with the lands set aside for his maintenance, had been confirmed to Lady Katherine, Hastings's widow, on 23 July 1483. *British Library Harleian Manuscript 433*, vol. 2, p. 5. The rest of the properties were administered by Varnam and his colleague, and, although custody of these was granted to

William Huse, chief justice of the King's Bench, on 13 April 1484, the only practical difference may have been that Varnam remitted the rents to Huse instead of to the Crown. *Calendar of the Patent Rolls, Edward IV, Edward V, Richard III, 1476-1485* (1901), pp. 391, 432. Edward was still a minor in February 1487 when Queen Elizabeth of York was granted an annuity of £100 from the revenues of his estates. W. Campbell (ed.), *Materials for a History of the Reign of Henry VII*, 2 vols (1873–7), vol. 2, p. 116. He died, leaving a daughter, in 1499.

CHAPTER SIX. THE COLCHESTER 'CONNECTION'

1. Some writers argue that Lovel was absent from the battle of Bosworth because the King had earlier sent him to Southampton to resist a Tudor landing on the south coast. But Richard knew that Henry was marching through Wales by 11 August (the day he summoned Henry Vernon and other potential supporters to join him at Nottingham), and may then have dispatched a messenger ordering Francis to return immediately. The distance from Nottingham to Southampton and from Southampton back to Leicester (where the *Great Chronicle of London* says that Lovel was in Richard's company on 21 August) is a little over 300 miles, and the messenger and Lovel could have covered this distance in the ten days available to them. It is also possible that Francis learned that Henry was making for Wales from mariners, and had decided to rejoin Richard before the royal summons arrived.

2. These paragraphs are based on G.H. Martin, *The Story of Colchester from Roman Times to the Present Day* (Colchester, 1959), especially ch. 3.

3. This section is based upon L.M. Higgs, *Godliness and Governance in Tudor Colchester* (Ann Arbor, 1998), pp.

58–9, and the *Victoria County History of Essex*, vol. 2, ed. W. Page and J. H. Round (1907), p. 97.

4. Abbot Sante said that 'ther must be a Lre [letter] left in maner as yt were lost, in the place where the said Erle shuld be, directed to some good felowe, that he shuld come unto theym to Colchester' (*Rotuli Parliamentorum*, ed. J. Strachey *et al.*, 6 vols (1767–77), vol. 6, p. 437). I am grateful to Peter Hammond for discussing the meaning of this with me.

5. Cleymound's role as a double agent was first argued by Wilhelm Busch, *England under the Tudors*, vol. 1, *King Henry VII* (1895), p. 120, but has since been questioned by Ian Arthurson, *The Perkin Warbeck Conspiracy 1491–1499* (Stroud, 1994), p. 207. Perhaps the real truth will never be known.

6. *Calendar of the Close Rolls, Edward IV, Edward V, Richard III, 1476–1485* (1954), pp. 339–40. Abbot Stansted was also summoned to attend Parliament on 15 November 1482 when Lovel was probably numbered with 'Ralph Greystok chavaler and 23 other chevalers' below the rank of Earl (*ibid.*, pp. 290–1).

7. We have no knowledge of Lovel's whereabouts between May 1486 and January 1487 (when he finally left for Burgundy), but Oxford was 'home territory' (only 16 miles from his seat at Minster Lovel), and he must have spent much of the interval encouraging the Simnel plot. See *The Paston Letters A.D. 1422–1509*, ed. J. Gairdner, 6 vols (1904), vol. 6, pp. 92–3, 95.

8. *Letters and Papers Illustrative of the Reigns of Richard III and Henry VII*, ed. J. Gairdner, 2 vols (1861–3), vol. 1, p. 234.

9. 'And my lord lovell come to grace than that ye shew to hym that he pray for me' (D. Williams, 'The Hastily Drawn up Will of William Catesby Esquire, 25 August

1485', *Transactions of the Leicestershire Archaeological and Historical Society*, 51 (1975–6), p. 48).

10. W. Campbell (ed.), *Materials for a History of the Reign of Henry VII*, 2 vols (1873–7), vol. 1, p. 228. Knighton was a confidential agent who was sent at various times to Berwick and Flanders. He was dead by 2 August 1500.

11. *Ibid.*, pp. 118–19, 171, 346. *Paston Letters*, vol. 6, p. 121.

12. Martin, *The Story of Colchester*, p. 43.

13. *Calendar of the Patent Rolls, Henry VII, 1485–1494* (1914), p. 341.

14. See E. Power, *Medieval People* (Harmondsworth, 1951), chs 4, 5.

15. I am grateful to Paul Coverley, Branch Archivist at the Colchester and N.E. Essex Branch of the Essex Record Office, for checking the Oath and Red Paper Books, and advising me accordingly. Eleanor's husband's name was certainly Thomas (see *passim*), and he is the only Thomas Kechyn of whom we know.

16. TNA: PRO C 1/144/55. I am grateful to Mrs Tina Hampson for locating this document and transcribing it for me.

17. The issue of such a writ did not presuppose that there was something wrong with the lower court's decision, only that the appellate court wished to re-examine it – but if an order of certiorari was issued then the lower court's actions could be reversed.

18. I am grateful to Ken Smallbone and Dr Richard Palmer, Librarian and Archivist at Lambeth Palace Library, for their advice on these matters.

CHAPTER SEVEN. IN THE SHADOWS

1. *The Anglica Historia of Polydore Vergil 1485–1537*, ed. D. Hay (Camden Society, 1950), p. 75.

2. *Ibid.*, p. 13.

3. *The Paston Letters A.D. 1422–1509*, ed. J. Gairdner, 6 vols (1904), vol. 6, pp. 91–2. *Register of the Great Seal of Scotland*, ed. J.B. Paul (Edinburgh, 1882), p. 370, no. 1738.

4. Francis Bacon, *The History of the Reign of King Henry VII*, ed. R. Lockyer (1971), p. 67.

5. The discovery is described by William Cowper, 'clerk of the Parliament', writing to Francis Peck in 1737. See G.E.C. *et al.*, *The Complete Peerage*, 12 vols (1910–59), vol. 8, p. 225.

6. D. Baldwin, *Stoke Field: The Last Battle of the Wars of the Roses* (Barnsley, 2006), pp. 87–8.

7. The legal deliberations are described in C.H. Williams, 'The Rebellion of Humphrey Stafford in 1486', *English Historical Review*, 43 (1928), pp. 181–9.

8. Vergil, *Anglica Historia*, p. 13.

9. Edward Halle, *The Union of the Two Noble Families of Lancaster and York* (1550; repr. Menston, 1970), 'The politique governaunce of Kyng Henry VII', fo. v (spelling modernised).

10. There is a short biography of Sante in A.B. Emden, *A Biographical Register of the University of Oxford to 1500*, 3 vols (Oxford, 1959), vol. 3, p. 1641.

11. *The York House Books 1461–1490*, ed. L.C. Attreed, 2 vols (Stroud, 1991), vol. 2, p. 737. For an excellent short biography of Stillington see *The Registers of Robert Stillington Bishop of Bath and Wells 1466–1491 and Richard Fox Bishop of Bath and Wells 1492–1494*, ed. Sir H.C. Maxwell-Lyte, Somerset Record Society 52 (1937), pp. viii–xv.

12. W. Campbell (ed.), *Materials for a History of the Reign of Henry VII*, 2 vols (1873–7), vol. 1, pp. 172–3.

13. The correspondence between the King and the masters is printed in *Epistolae Academicae Oxon.*, ed. H. Anstey, 2 vols (Oxford, 1898), vol. 2, pp. 513–23.

14. *Registers of Robert Stillington*, p. xiii.
15. The phrase is Paul Murray Kendall's (*Richard III* (1973), p. 475).
16. Bacon, *Henry VII*, p. 60.
17. The prime example is Henry's mother, Lady Margaret Beaufort, who could have 'retired' after her son's victory, but who instead became one of his chief political advisers and wealthier than she had ever been in the past.
18. This is discussed in D. Baldwin, *Elizabeth Woodville: Mother of the Princes in the Tower* (Stroud, 2002), p. 124.
19. This section is based on M.K. Jones and M.G. Underwood, *The King's Mother* (Cambridge, 1992), pp. 126, 134, 162.
20. A.F. Pollard, *The Reign of Henry VII from Contemporary Sources*, 3 vols (1913–14), vol. 2, p. 4.
21. N.H. Nicolas, *Privy Purse Expenses of Elizabeth of York: Wardrobe Accounts of Edward IV* (1830; repr. 1972).
22. Bacon, *Henry VII*, p. 64.
23. Halle, *The Union*, 'The politique governaunce of Kyng Henry VII', fo. ix.
24. J.R. Lander, *Crown and Nobility* (1976), pp. 286–8.
25. T.B. Pugh, writing in the *Oxford Dictionary of National Biography*, 60 vols (Oxford, 2004), vol. 23, p. 880.
26. Professor Lander notes that the Earl of Devon and eight others put up mainprises for Dorset's allegiance totalling £2,766 13s 4d in September 1496. They were not, apparently, substitutes for some of the earlier guarantors, so it is possible that a new arrangement had been substituted for the old. Lander, *Crown and Nobility*, p. 288.
27. *The Chronicle of Calais to the Year 1540*, ed. J.G. Nichols (Camden Society, 1846), p. 6.
28. *Letters and Papers Illustrative of the Reigns of Richard III and Henry VII*, ed. J. Gairdner, 2 vols (1861–3), vol. 1, p. 233.

29. Vergil, *Anglica Historia*, p. 27.
30. Bacon, *Henry VII*, p. 64.
31. This section is based on the article on Edmund in the *Oxford Dictionary of National Biography*, vol. 44, pp. 696–8.
32. *Letters and Papers*, ed. Gairdner, vol. 1, p. 258.
33. The only de la Pole brother who outlived Richard was William, born *c.* 1478, who was arrested in 1502 and spent the rest of his life in the Tower. He was alive as late as October 1539, but had died, apparently, by November 1540. He had surely long since ceased to pose any threat to the Tudor dynasty – unless, of course, he knew of the 'lost prince'.
34. Vergil, *Anglica Historia*, p. 17.
35. See A. Wroe, *Perkin: A Story of Deception* (2004), p. 369.
36. *Calendar of the Patent Rolls, Henry VII, 1485–1494* (1914), p. 26.
37. Ann Wroe points out that, if Curteys took Warbeck seriously, 'he was not altogether certain, therefore, that Edward's second son was dead' (*Perkin*, p. 438).
38. This section is based on *The Estate and Household Accounts of William Worsley, Dean of St Paul's Cathedral 1479–1497*, ed. H. Kleineke and S.R. Hovland (2004), pp. 3–17.

CHAPTER EIGHT. 'COUSIN' HENRY

1. *Letters and Papers, Foreign and Domestic, of the Reign of Henry VIII 1509–47*, ed. J.S. Brewer, J. Gairdner and R.H. Brodie, 21 vols. (1862–1910), vol. 1, p. 522. TNA: PRO C 66/61.
2. Arthur adopted the name 'Plantagenet' only after the Plantagenets no longer ruled England. The difference is that he was public knowledge and Richard was not.

3. The 'Building Accounts of Kirby Muxloe Castle' (ed., with an introduction and notes, A.H. Thompson, *Transactions of the Leicestershire Archaeological Society*, 11 (1915)) show that professional bricklayers doubled as labourers on occasion according to need.

4. *British Library Harleian Manuscript 433*, ed. R. Horrox and P.W. Hammond, 4 vols (Upminster and London 1979–83), vol. 2, p. 96.

5. Quoted by A.L. Bedingfeld, *A Cartulary of Creake Abbey* (Norfolk Record Society, 1966), p. xxii. The brass of Sir William now in North Creake church may have come from the abbey.

6. *Ibid*. Aslak also bequeathed a complete vestment of white damask to the abbot and five shillings to each canon, the whole on condition that they remembered his obit.

7. *Ibid*., p. xxi. The 'sweating sickness' has also been blamed, but events at Creake do not coincide with the known major outbreaks of the illness in 1485 and 1508.

8. The bricklayers who built Kirby Muxloe Castle for William, Lord Hastings, in the early 1480s – Mark Maligoo, Staner Matlot, Charlot Ruddicourt, Turkyn Horwynd and Arnold Ruskyn – were probably all Flemings. A. Hamilton Thompson writes that 'it is probably a safe conjecture that they were craftsmen, originally from the Low Countries, who exercised their trade in East Anglia and were imported from that centre of brick architecture to work at Hastings' new masterpiece' (Thompson (ed.), 'The Building Accounts of Kirby Muxloe Castle 1480–1484', p. 205). It would not have been long before native Englishmen learned the craft too.

9. J.L. Fisher, 'The Leger Book of St John's Abbey Colchester', *Transactions of the Essex Archaeological Society*, NS 24 (1944–9), pp. 114–15.

10. *Letters and Papers Henry VIII*, vol. 9, p. 383.
11. Surrey's father, the Duke of Norfolk, was also condemned, but Henry VIII died the night before he was to be executed and in the resulting uncertainty his life was spared.
12. The fullest biography of Margaret Pole is by Hazel Pierce, *Margaret Pole Countess of Salisbury 1473–1541* (2003).
13. Quoted by J.J. Scarisbrick, *Henry VIII* (Yale, 1997), p. 383.
14. *Ibid.*, p. 382.
15. A surname he shared with Richard, who, it must be assumed, abandoned 'Grey' much as Arthur did 'Wayte'.
16. These paragraphs are based on C. Given-Wilson and A. Curteis, *The Royal Bastards of Medieval England* (1984), pp. 162–73. A selection from Arthur's correspondence has been printed as *The Lisle Letters*, ed. M. St Clare Byrne, 6 vols. (1981).
17. For an excellent, more detailed, summary of these events see R. Rex, *The Tudors* (Stroud, 2003), especially pp. 57–98.
18. Quoted in the *Victoria County History of Essex*, ed. W. Page and J.H. Round, vol. 2 (1907), p. 97. This section is based upon pp. 97–100.
19. *Letters and Papers Henry VIII*, vol. 14, p. 120.
20. Quoted in *VCH Essex*, vol. 2, pp. 98–9.
21. *Ibid.*, pp. 98, 100.
22. *Ibid.*, p. 100.
23. For an excellent short account of the likely fate of the religious and others see G. Baskerville, *English Monks and the Suppression of the Monasteries* (1965), especially ch. x and pp. 285–7.

CHAPTER NINE. KING RICHARD IV?

1. *Rotuli Parliamentorum*, ed. J. Strachey *et al.*, 6 vols. (1767–77), vol. 6, p. 276.

2. Some writers argue that the boys posed a more serious threat to Henry than they had to King Richard and he would have been well-nigh obliged to kill them if they were still living in August 1485. But such arguments disregard both family pressures and considerations, and the alternative solution of giving both or one of them a new persona and a new life.

3. Their efforts to comfort one another when they were informed of the death of their eldest son Prince Arthur in April 1502 suggest that their relationship was by then much more that the marriage of convenience it had been at the outset. See D. Baldwin, *Elizabeth Woodville: Mother of the Princes in the Tower* (Stroud, 2002), pp. 151–2.

4. D. Baldwin, *Stoke Field: The Last Battle of the Wars of the Roses* (Barnsley, 2006), pp. 87–8.

5. Richard's slightly bowed head seems to be focused on the tomb effigy of William Warham, Archbishop of Canterbury from 1503 to 1532, in the chapel below. However, it must be remembered that the 'royal window' may not now be in its original location (it was probably lower, at the bottom, in the usual donor's position), and that the heads of some of the figures have been replaced.

APPENDIX ONE. RICHARD PLANTAGENET: A LEGENDARY TALE

1. This is a common mistake. There can be no *bar sinister*, as a bar in heraldry is a horizontal division of the shield. It should be 'bend', 'bendlet' or 'baton' sinister, but even that is incorrect for this explanation, as a bend sinister goes from right to left. (I am indebted to Geoffrey Wheeler for this observation.)

APPENDIX TWO. SOME JOURNALISTIC ASIDES

1. A known pseudonym of Dr Samuel Pegge, the antiquary.

2. A. Wagner, *Heralds and Ancestors* (1928). I am indebted to Geoffrey Wheeler for this reference.

APPENDIX THREE. THE HOPPER RING

1. *Illustrated London News*, 4 October 1856, p. 35.
2. Dr Brett had written that Richard of Eastwell lived with his Latin schoolmaster until he was 'fifteen or sixteen' (F. Peck, *Desiderata Curiosa*, vol. 2 (1779), p. 250).
3. A. Cartwright, 'Research Notes and Queries', *The Ricardian*, 5 (1981), pp. 403–4.
4. I am indebted to Marilyn Garabet for this reference.
5. The story was told by Mrs Daniel to some visiting members of the Kent branch of the Richard III Society in 1989 and reported by Vera Blackman in their magazine *White Surrey* in October that year. The article suggests that it was Mrs Daniel who asked her nephews for permission to place the ring in her late husband's museum, but it certainly formed part of the collection when Mr Daniel was alive.
6. I am indebted to Doug Weeks and Philippa Langley for this information.
7. Letter from Mrs E.A. Bouchard, administrator at Lennoxlove House Ltd, to Marilyn Garabet, 29 March 1994.

# Select Bibliography

The place of publication is London unless otherwise stated.

*Archive Material*
The National Archives (TNA): Public Record Office (PRO)
  TNA: PRO C 1/144/55
  TNA: PRO C 66/61


*Published Works*
Alles, A., 'Heraldry in Medieval England', in P. Coss and M. Keen (eds), *Heraldry, Pageantry and Social Display in Medieval England* (2002)
Aston, M., and Horrox, R. (eds), *Much Heaving and Shoving: Essays for Colin Richmond* (2005)
Auden, T., *Shrewsbury: A Historical and Topographical Account of the Town* (1905)
Bacon, Francis, *The History of the Reign of King Henry VII*, ed. R. Lockyer (1971)
Baldwin, D., *Elizabeth Woodville: Mother of the Princes in the Tower* (Stroud, 2002)
——, *Stoke Field: The Last Battle of the Wars of the Roses* (Barnsley, 2006)
Barnfield, M., 'Richard and Anne's Dispensation', *Ricardian Bulletin* (Spring 2006)
Baskerville, G., *English Monks and the Suppression of the Monasteries* (1965)
Bedingfeld, A.L., *A Cartulary of Creake Abbey* (Norfolk Record Society, 1966)

Bedingfeld, A.L., and Gilyard-Beer, R., *Creake Abbey* (HMSO, 1970)

Begent, P.J., and Chesshyre, H., *The Most Noble Order of the Garter: 650 Years* (1999)

Bentley, S. (ed.), *Excerpta Historica or Illustrations of English History* (1831)

Bishop, R.C., 'Richard Plantagenet of Eastwell – Fact or Fiction', *The Ricardian*, 3 (1974)

*British Library Harliean Manuscript 433*, ed. R. Horrox and P.W. Hammond, 4 vols (Upminster and London, 1979–83)

Buck, Sir George, *The History of King Richard the Third*, ed. A.N. Kincaid (Gloucester, 1979)

Busch, W., *England under the Tudors*, vol. 1, *King Henry VII* (1895)

*Calendar of the Close Rolls, Edward IV, Edward V, Richard III, 1476–1485* (1954)

*Calendar of the Patent Rolls, Edward IV, Edward V, Richard III, 1476–1485* (1901)

*Calendar of the Patent Rolls, Henry VII, 1485–1494* (1914)

Cartwright, A., 'Research Notes and Queries', *The Ricardian*, 5 (1981)

*The Chronicle of Calais to the Year 1540*, ed. J.G. Nichols (Camden Society, 1846)

*The Chronicles of the White Rose of York*, ed. J.C. Giles (1845)

Coss, P., and Keen, M. (eds), *Heraldry, Pageantry and Social Display in Medieval England* (2002)

Councer, C.R., 'The Medieval and Renaissance Painted Glass of Eastwell', *Archaeologia Cantiana*, 59 (1946)

Crawford, A., 'The Mowbray Inheritance', in J. Petre (ed.), *Richard III: Crown and People* (Gloucester, 1985)

*The Crowland Chronicle Continuations 1459–1486*, ed. N. Pronay and J. Cox (1986)

Davies, R. (ed.), *Extracts from the Municipal Records of the City of York during the Reigns of Edward IV, Edward V and Richard III* (1843)

D'Elboux, R.H., 'Some Kentish Indents', *Archaeologia Cantiana*, 59 (1946)

Dening, J., *Secret History: The Truth about Richard III and the Princes* (Brandon, 1996)

*Dictionary of National Biography*, ed. L. Stephen and S. Lee, 63 vols (1885–1900)

Dockray, K., *Richard III: A Source Book* (Stroud, 1997)

*Domesday Book. Kent*, ed. P. Morgan (Chichester, 1983)

Dormer, P.G., *Eastwell Park Historiette* (Eastwell Park, 1999)

Emden, A.B., *A Biographical Register of the University of Oxford to 1500*, 3 vols (Oxford, 1959)

*An English Chronicle of the Reigns of Richard II, Henry IV, Henry V, and Henry VI*, ed. J.S. Davies (Camden Society, 1856)

*Epistolae Academicae Oxon.*, ed. H. Anstey, 2 vols (Oxford, 1898)

*The Estate and Household Accounts of William Worsley, Dean of St Paul's Cathedral 1479–1497*, ed. H. Kleineke and S.R. Hovland (2004)

Fields, B., *Royal Blood* (New York, 1998)

Fisher, J.L., 'The Leger Book of St John's Abbey Colchester', *Transactions of the Essex Archaeological Society*, NS 24 (1944–9)

G.E.C. *et al.*, *The Complete Peerage*, 12 vols (1910–59)

*Gentleman's Magazine*, vol. 37 (1767)

Given-Wilson, C., and Curteis, A., *The Royal Bastards of Medieval England* (1984)

*The Great Chronicle of London*, ed. A.H. Thomas and I.D. Thornley (1938; repr. Gloucester, 1983)

Halle, Edward, *The Union of the Two Noble Families of Lancaster and York* (1550; reprinted Menston, 1970)

Halliwell, J.O. (ed.), *Letters of the Kings of England*, 2 vols (1846)

Hammond, P.W., 'The Illegitimate Children of Richard III', in J. Petre (ed.), *Richard III: Crown and People* (Gloucester, 1985)

Hanham, A., *Richard III and his Early Historians 1483–1535* (Oxford, 1975)

——, 'Sir George Buck and Princess Elizabeth's Letter: A Problem in Detection', *The Ricardian*, 7 (1987)

Hepburn, F., *Portraits of the Later Plantagenets* (1986)

Hicks, M., *Anne Neville: Queen to Richard III* (Stroud, 2006)

——, *Edward V: The Prince in the Tower* (Stroud, 2003)

——, *False, Fleeting, Perjur'd Clarence 1449–78* (Bangor, 1992)

——, *Richard III* (Stroud, 2000)

Higgs, L.M., *Godliness and Governance in Tudor Colchester* (Ann Arbor, 1998)

*Historie of the Arrivall of Edward IV in England and the Finall Recouerye of His Kingdomes from Henry VI, A.D. M.CCCC.LXXI*, ed. J. Bruce (Camden Society, 1846)

Igglesden, C., *A Saunter through Kent with Pen and Pencil*, vol. 3 (Ashford, 1901)

*Ingulph's Chronicle of the Abbey of Croyland*, trans. H.T. Riley (1854)

Jones, M.K., and Underwood, M.G., *The King's Mother* (Cambridge, 1992)

Kendall, P.M., *Richard III* (1955, 1973)

Kleyn, D.M., *Richard of England* (1990)

Lander, J.R., *Crown and Nobility* (1976)

Leland, J., *De Rebus Britannicis Collectanea*, ed. T. Hearne, 6 vols (1770)

*Letters and Papers, Foreign and Domestic, of the Reign of Henry VIII 1509–47*, ed. J.S. Brewer, J. Gairdner and R.H. Brodie, 21 vols (1862–1910)

*Letters and Papers Illustrative of the Reigns of Richard III and Henry VII*, ed. J. Gairdner, 2 vols (1861–3)

*The Lisle Letters*, ed. M. St Clare Byrne, 6 vols (1981)

Lulofs, M., 'Richard III: Dutch Sources', *The Ricardian*, 3 (1974)

Madden, F., 'Documents Relating to Perkin Warbeck, with Remarks on his History', *Archaeologia*, 27 (1838)

Mancini, Dominic, *The Usurpation of Richard III*, trans. C.A.J. Armstrong (Oxford, 1969; repr. Gloucester, 1984)

Martin, G.H., *The Story of Colchester from Roman Times to the Present Day* (Colchester, 1959)

*Materials for a History of the Reign of Henry VII*, ed. W. Campbell, 2 vols (1873–7)

Merriam, T., 'John Clement: His Identity and his Marshfoot House in Essex', *Moreana*, 25 (1988)

Morant, Philip, *The History and Antiquities of the Most Ancient Town and Borough of Colchester* (1748; repr. Wakefield, 1970)

More, Thomas, *More's History of King Richard III*, ed. J.R. Lumby (Cambridge, 1883)

——, *More's Utopia*, ed. J.R. Lumby (Cambridge, 1908)

——, *The History of King Richard III*, ed. R.S. Sylvester (New Haven, 1976)

Moreton, C.E., 'A Local Dispute and the Politics of 1483: Roger Townshend, Earl Rivers and the Duke of Gloucester', *The Ricardian*, 7 (1989)

Myers, A.R. (ed.), *The Household of Edward IV: The Black Book and the Ordinance of 1478* (Manchester, 1959)

'Narrative of the Marriage of Richard Duke of York with Anne of Norfolk: The Matrimonial Feast and the Grand Jousting', in W.H. Black (ed.), *Illustrations of Ancient State and Chivalry from Manuscripts Preserved in the Ashmolean Museum* (Roxburghe Club, 1840)

Nicolas, N.H., *Privy Purse Expenses of Elizabeth of York: Wardrobe Accounts of Edward IV* (1830)

Nichols, W.B., *The Secret Son* (Leicester, 1944)

Norman, G., 'How Holbein Hid a Royal Secret', *The Times*, Friday 25 March 1983

*Notes and Queries*, 4th series, 6 (31 December 1870)

*Oxford Dictionary of National Biography*, ed. H.C.G. Matthew and B. Harrison, 60 vols (Oxford, 2004)

Parkin, E.W., 'The Vanishing Houses of Kent. 8. Lake House, Eastwell', *Archaeologia Cantiana*, 83 (1968)

*The Paston Letters A.D. 1422–1509*, ed. J. Gairdner, 6 vols (1904)

Peck, F., *Desiderata Curiosa*, vol. 2 (1779)

Pierce, H., *Margaret Pole Countess of Salisbury 1473–1541* (2003)

Pollard, A.F., *The Reign of Henry VII from Contemporary Sources*, 3 vols (1913–14)

Pollard, A.J., *Richard III and the Princes in the Tower* (Stroud, 1991).

Power, E., *Medieval People* (Harmondsworth, 1951)

*Register of the Great Seal of Scotland*, ed. J.B. Paul (Edinburgh, 1882)

*The Registers of Robert Stillington Bishop of Bath and Wells 1466–1491 and Richard Fox Bishop of Bath and Wells 1492–1494*, ed. Sir H.C. Maxwell-Lyte, Somerset Record Society 52 (1937)

Rex, R., *The Tudors* (Stroud, 2003)

Ross, C., *Richard III* (1981)

*Rotuli Parliamentorum*, ed. J. Strachey *et al.*, 6 vols (1767–77)

Scofield, C.L., *The Life and Reign of Edward the Fourth*, 2 vols (1923)

Scarisbrick, J.J., *Henry VIII* (Yale, 1997)

Smith, G., 'Lambert Simnel and the King from Dublin', *The Ricardian*, 10 (1996)

Steele, R. (ed), *Kings' Letters* (1903)

*The Stonor Letters and Papers*, ed. C.L. Kingsford, 2 vols (Camden Society, 1919)

Sutton, A.F., and Visser-Fuchs, L., *Richard III's Books* (Stroud, 1997)

Thompson, A. H. (ed., with an introduction and notes), 'The Building Accounts of Kirby Muxloe Castle 1480–1484', *Transactions of the Leicestershire Archaeological Society*, 11 (1915)

Throsby, John, *Select Views in Leicestershire* (1789)

Vergil, Polydore, *The Anglica Historia of Polydore Vergil 1485–1537*, ed. D. Hay (Camden Society, 1950)

——, *Three Books of Polydore Vergil's English History*, ed. H. Ellis (Camden Society, 1844)

*The Victoria County History of Essex*, ed. W. Page and J.H. Round, vol. 2 (1907)

Visser-Fuchs, L., 'Where did Elizabeth of York find Consolation?', *The Ricardian*, 9 (1993)

Wagner, A., *Heralds and Ancestors* (1928)

Warkworth, John, *A Chronicle of the First Thirteen Years of the Reign of King Edward the Fourth*, ed. J.O. Halliwell (Camden Society, 1839)

Wedgwood, J.C., *History of Parliament*, vol. 1, *Biographies* (1936)

Weir, A., *The Princes in the Tower* (1992)

Williams, C.H., 'The Rebellion of Humphrey Stafford in 1486', *English Historical Review*, 43 (1928)

Williams, D., 'The Hastily Drawn up Will of William Catesby Esquire, 25 August 1485', *Transactions of the Leicestershire Archaeological and Historical Society*, 51 (1975–6)

Williamson, A., *The Mystery of the Princes* (Dursley, 1978)

Wroe, A., *Perkin: A Story of Deception* (2004)

——, 'From Ann Wroe', in 'Who Was Perkin Warbeck', *Ricardian Bulletin* (Summer 2005)

*The York House Books 1461–1490*, ed. L. C. Attreed, 2 vols (Stroud, 1991)

# *Index*

# Index

Made in the USA
Monee, IL
02 April 2023

31069880R00144